UNDERSTANDING

CAPITALISM

How economies work

Brian Kantor

BRIEFINGS
Series Editor: Peter Collins

BOYARS/BOWERDEAN
LONDON. NEW YORK

First published in 1995 jointly by
the Bowerdean Publishing Co. Ltd., 8 Abbotstone Rd, London SW15 1QR
and Marion Boyars Publishers, 24 Lacy Rd., London SW15 1NL
and 237 East 39th St., New York, NY 10016
Distributed in Australia and New Zealand by
Peribo Pty Ltd, 58 Beaumont Road, Mount Kuring-gai, NSW 2080

British Library Cataloguing in Publication Data

Kantor, Brian
Understanding Capitalism:How Economies
Work. - (Briefings Series)
I. Title II. Series
330.122

Library of Congress Cataloging-in-Publication Data

Kantor, Brian
  Understanding capitalism : how economies work / by Brian Kantor.
      p.   cm. -- (Briefings)
  1. Capitalism. 2. Economics. I. Title. II. Series: Briefings
(London, England)
HB501.K245 1995
330.12\2--dc20   94-31506
                                                  CIP

Original Paperback

Designed and typeset by Bowerdean Publishing Co. Ltd.
Printed and bound in Great Britain by Itchen Printers Ltd., Southampton.

ISBN 0-7145- 2973- 7

CONTENTS

DEDICATION

For Shirley, Charles and Daniel who have always given me a sense of worth in the work I do. Even more than that, they have never been economical with their love.

Acknowledgments

Peter Collins suggested I write this book and I am very glad he did so. I expected him to be a challenging and demanding editor which would be very good for the book. He has contributed every bit as well as expected. I valued his critical efforts on my behalf and appreciated even more his approval of what I was doing. My friend David Matthews has played a vital role in this enterprise. With his passion for reading, thinking hard and taking trouble with ideas, he provided an ideal sounding board as the practical businessman I wished to reach. He made a great many suggestions to improve on my original efforts and made it absolutely clear to me what was not obvious to him. I tried hard to come more clearly to the point, and if I have succeeded better in doing so, he deserves much of the credit.

The book was largely written while I was on sabbatical leave from the School of Economics of the University of Cape Town. This was spent at the Graduate School of Business of Columbia University, New York. I would like to thank both universities for providing me with the time to write. Stern-Stewart and Company of New York did much to make my highly stimulating time at Columbia possible and I would very much like to recognize their contribution.

Brian Kantor
Professor of Economics
University of Cape Town
South Africa

PREFACE

The Aim

This book is written for those who are interested in understanding what is going on in the economy for good business reasons. They are likely to regard the business and economic commentary in the newspapers they read as at least as important as the front or the sports pages. They will also read the more specialized business journals both because they are deeply interested in the subject matter and because it is necessary for them to be well informed about economic events and economic policy.

I hope the book will give them a deeper insight into the economic issues and events that are bound to confront them in business. It may also help them in their social lives at times when they may be called upon to make a comment on some burning issue of the day when their side, that of business, seems to be off-side, and they have to justify some apparent act of economic cruelty. It is surely important for those in business to understand the "big picture" and how they fit into it. They and others should appreciate why the careful management of resources, which is what successful businesses do, is so important for society. A popular phrase of the moment is "tough love". The insights economists bring are perhaps the most important example of tough love. They tell of the huge advantages a realistic but seemingly hard hearted approach to the economy has brought and will bring to the least well-off people among us.

The book will have achieved its objectives if readers are made not only more aware of, and understand better, the economic forces at work, but are able to make improved predictions about economic growth rates, and about inflation and exchange and interest rates and developments in financial markets generally. .

The study of economics is no longer quite the dismal science it was when economies were so much smaller and the bounds of nature so much more important. If the book has a moral lesson to impart, it is that if societies fail to seize the economic development opportunities available to them, the kind of opportunities that have been taken elsewhere, the fault is in themselves and not in their stars.

My own belief is that economic freedom, that is, freedom from government restrictions on acts of exchange that economic actors wish to undertake, is both desirable for its own sake and because such freedom helps deliver the goods. The book will provide evidence for this position and if by so doing it encourages a belief in economic freedom, so much the better. However, the purpose of the book is not to convince the reader of the virtues of one economic system compared to another. The object of the exercise is to help the reader predict the performance of a modern market-oriented economy, for good business reasons.

The US economy provides most of the examples that are used to illustrate the analysis. But the issues, as will be recognized, are universal. It would be a simple matter to replace the examples taken from the US economy with cases from other economies. Nevertheless, the USA remains the giant among economies, in a world economy that is becoming more and more closely integrated. Knowledge of how the US economy works is important for understanding economic developments everywhere.

The book is not an academic exercise, where as much as possible of what is said is supported by as many references as possible to previous authority. It represents what my own thoughts are with as much power of reasoning as I can muster, to assist the reader, who is not expected to be a professional economist (though I certainly do hope that my fellow economists will find merit in what I have done). If I fail to convince, it is all my own fault. I have come to the positions I take with the assistance of many others, only a few of whom are mentioned here. A small number of references are made, perhaps too many, to schools of thought and books and articles that could assist in further exploration.

The Direction

The economic short-run is dominated by phases of faster and slower growth, described as the business cycle. An appreciation of the longer-run growth potential of the economy is vital if we are to predict what is likely to happen with the economy over the next year or two. And so attention is given to the *supply side*[1] of the economy, i.e. the forces making for faster or slower growth over the long term. An economy responds in predictable ways to the pressures of above or below average growth. An analysis and interpretation is provided, of how excessive pressures on the capacity of the economy to produce more are relieved, and how the economy might be expected to react to any failure to employ available resources. The role financial markets play in matching supply and demand is very important and receives much attention. The methods and influence on the economy of the Treasury, or Ministry of Finance, with powers over taxes and government spending, and of the Central Bank with responsibilities for interest and exchange rates and the supply of money, have a great bearing on how the economy will behave and are the focus of much discussion.

The book is ordered in the following way: Chapters 1 to 4 deal with some of the big issues, the forces that make for the wealth or poverty of nations. The attempt is made to demonstrate an economist's way of looking at the world and the validity of this approach. A number of economic issues that might confront the reader are presented to illustrate the analysis.

Chapters 5 to 13 are more obviously practical with the focus on understanding the likely performance of the economy. A perspective on the policies that are used to manage total spending or demand in the economy is provided in

Chapter 5. The failure of the attempt to unify monetary policies in Europe is examined to illustrate the issues.

Chapter 6 explains how economic growth is measured and some of the ambiguities of such measures are also considered there.

Chapter 7 identifies the important economic trends to look out for when deciding whether an economy is about to gather or lose economic strength over the long term.

The economic role played by participants in financial markets and why they react to economic events the way they do are given close scrutiny in Chapter 8.

In Chapter 9, the nature of financial and business risk and its management is given close attention.

Some of the essential features of the business cycle are identified in Chapter 10.

Chapter 11 delves further into the forces acting on exchange rates and policies for international trade.

The reactions of monetary policy to the business cycle and the influence of monetary policy on the business cycle are the focus of chapter 12.

The important role played by expectations receives much attention in the concluding Chapter 13.

1. I have tried to alert readers to the jargon of economists and economic journalists, in so far as I am capable of recognizing it, with appropriate italics. The meaning should be clear.

CHAPTER ONE

TRADE-OFFS

Or how to spoil the party by inviting an economist

There are very few people who do not wish for more of what they regard as the good things in life. Even when, by any objective standards, they are living well, many objects of their desire – for a better house or car, a superior education for their children, to give more to a noble cause – will be frustrated. This frustration is known as the *economic problem*. Nature by itself is not generous enough to give us everything and we are forced to make do with less. We have to limit our consumption demands because we do not produce enough output and so earn enough income. Nor do our fellow citizens, upon whose production we might make claim. The economic problem is mostly the result of limited production, a *supply side* problem. At times though, an economic system will deliver less than it can because of a lack of co-ordination between demand and supply. These issues are addressed when we consider the business cycle.

The economic problem is that producing more of one kind of output means that less can be supplied of any other kind. Quite simply, more food, shelter or medicine made available to one family will mean less for others. Society and individuals are forced to choose between competing claims on their scarce productive resources; more of this for less of that, more for him, less for her. Every society is forced to make these *trade-offs* or economic compromises.

Any society with material objectives will also have to acknowledge the relationship between what individuals produce for the economy, their economic contributions, and what they are allowed to keep for themselves and their families. Or in other words, groups of people with some common purpose and interest that make up a society are forced to recognize the importance of material incentives if economic growth and an improved general standard of living is an objective. Nevertheless, even where the principle of unequal rewards for unequal efforts is conceded, as it has to be if economic progress is to be made, there will always be public concern about the appropriateness of the economic incentives on offer. Any economic system will be under constant scrutiny for its ability to satisfy sentiments about fairness, as well as the concern for greater output.

Some would regard it as a matter of regret that material rewards for material effort are at all necessary. They regard giving as better than receiving. Others regard anything other than willing acts of exchange as the basis for organizing economic life, as morally illegitimate. All societies find themselves caught between the extremes, relying neither completely on consent, nor on force exercised by governments, to get their economic way. And this balancing act will be very important in determining the performance of their economies.

Economists are trained to reveal stark facts of life which, when they do so, tend to make them less than universally loved. They are messengers with bad news. Others – politicians, priests, lobbyists – sales people of all persuasions, emphasize how much more could be made available. They point to the benefits which might flow from spending on some desirable course, or of refraining from spending on something undesirable. They emphasize the joys of receiving. Economists try to establish what has to be given up and by whom if, what may be agreed are desirable objectives are to be realized. Their emphasis is on the less – what it all costs, what has to be paid for the goodies and by whom. They observe that people do not usually regard it as better to give than to receive. Economics was once regarded as "the dismal science" for the obvious reason that the choices open to society seemed so limited − a case of a little of this, for even less of that. With the material abundance now to be found in a number of countries, this description no longer seems appropriate. Economists offer more hope. Economics is now perhaps better described as the study of material choice and opportunity .

Ideally, the economic scientist should not be concerned with a society's economic goals or methods, but with explaining what is going on and why we observe the economic results we do.

Some examples of difficult economic choices

1) *About protecting the environment*
Clearly nobody particularly enjoys a polluted atmosphere or a noisy environment, which is why space on the noisy streets and in the dirty neighbourhoods attracts a town's lowest rents. The people who live or work there implicitly accept more noise, or dirtier air, as the price to be paid for lower transport costs and more food or more pay. Keeping out or closing down a polluting steel plant, while possibly enhancing property values in the immediate neighborhood, may mean a smaller tax base for the city, which may lead to higher city tax rates. This in turn will tend to force up wages or prices to cover the higher taxes and the result may be less local employment. The workers who used to live cheaply near the old plant will be forced to seek jobs and accommodation elsewhere.

There is a price to be paid for preventing the construction of new apartments on a beautiful mountain or beach. The land, if left in its pristine state, will be less productive of income and of income and other taxes. The trade-off for the community is the benefit of the greater income from the land in exchange for the view. If the owners could charge for a view of the unspoiled beach, as easily as they are able to charge for the view from the apartments overlooking it, the dispute between the competing claims of those for and against the development might be more easily resolved. A price can only be charged when potential consumers can be excluded from the benefits in some technically and economically feasible way. If prices are to be the mechanism for matching supply and demand, the system of charging must be not only technically feasible but politically acceptable. The right to charge must be available to the owner of some potentially valuable resource.

Similarly, it is not always possible to charge for the full costs of some activity. It is not feasible to compensate the listener for the damage caused by the noisy vehicle passing by, or for the damage to lungs caused by smoke in the air. Similarly the destruction of the forests may well increase the dangers of skin cancer but it is impossible to link the one act with the other. In both cases if there were reliable and inexpensive ways of assessing the damage and its cause, appropriate charges might be made. Some goods or services would become much more expensive if they were required to cover all their costs of production. Others would become cheaper if they were not burdened by taxes that go to pay for the government's clean-up operations. And so the economy's mix of demand and supply would be different in response to a different set of prices, if the technology for charging was available and was accompanied by the necessary political will.

In the absence of full information about who is responsible for the costs and who receives the benefits, society copes with these problems by either granting or withdrawing rights. You are tacitly given the right to pollute, or to make noise, or denied it. There are two equivalent solutions for reducing the damage. The owner of the car or the plane or the plant may be called upon to pay for the emission controls judged appropriate, or can be granted a subsidy to achieve the same objective environmental standard. The outcome – less pollution – will be the same. The only important difference is in who will have paid for the improvement. That is, do we prevent the activity? Or do we tax others and pay the polluters not to carry on that way, by providing them with a subsidy to cover the costs of cleaning up? [1]

The USA has recently allowed companies to buy and sell their obligations to reduce undesirable emissions. As an alternative to reducing their own pollution, firms can pay other firms in their neighbourhood to reduce pollutants below mandated levels. In this way the goal of achieving some pre-determined target for pollution can be achieved at lower total cost. The firms best able to reduce pollution are rewarded for doing so. They are better off, provided the amount they are paid by other firms to reduce their emissions by some volume below the target level exceeds their own costs of doing so. Similarly, the firm with high costs of reducing emissions will benefit, if what they pay is less than what it would cost them to reduce their own emissions by an equivalent volume. It is very much the economists' solution – a lower cost method of meeting some well defined objective.

The people in high income countries who are worried about the rain forests in the tropics, because they care about the air they breathe, or their vulnerability to ultraviolet rays (having long since destroyed their own forests), can deal with their anxieties in one of two ways. They could recognize the rights of the owners of the rain forest in the tropics and buy up their logging rights and maintain the jungle in its natural state. Similarly, they could compensate the logging companies in their own countries for ceasing to operate in order to preserve more of the forest in its natural state. However, what they are more likely to do, is to use the political process to alter the structure of rights to harvest timber. Their poor tropical neighbours in the global village, or much more likely, the local forestry companies, may simply be forced to shut down, without the offer of any compensation for their loss of income.

If the object of government intervention is conservation rather than expropriation, the mere danger of being shut down, of losing the right to farm or fish or generally extract, will tend to lead to a faster rate of exploitation of any natural resource and so prove counterproductive The hunter, or the fisherman, or the herder grazing livestock on the commons have no interest in conservation. They know that anything of value that they leave behind will be exploited by somebody else. And so they hunt, fish, or graze as if there were no tomorrow. The most obvious way to encourage the conservation of resources is to give secure rights of ownership to them. Enclosing the commons or the forest meant that their owners had the incentive to consider the influence of what they did today on what they would be able to harvest next year. This encouraged them to take the long view, in their own interests, and to conserve their resources accordingly. The yield from the land was then sustained at a much higher rate over time.

But the act of enclosure, while encouraging more output, to the great benefit of those given rights of ownership, also takes something away from those who previously enjoyed access to the commonly owned resource. Historically, the usual form of gaining ownership over the commons was through invasion and the exercise of force. Alternatively, the members of the tribe exchanged their rights as hunters and gatherers with the feudal lord, in return for protection against some other invader.

In many parts of the world, and especially in parts of Africa, the land under tribal authority remains subject to all the abuse and wasted output that results from common ownership. Clearly, conversion of the land to private ownership would enhance incomes from it over the long run. But finding an acceptable way to compensate those with traditional rights to the land for giving them up, as well as persuading them to respect new rights of ownership, remains a problem.

Unless the issue can be resolved, the land will remain relatively unproductive. Recycling left-overs, rather than filling up holes with them, may waste more resources, labor and fuel than the recycled materials are worth. This is why we generally fill up the garbage cans and then the land or the sea with our waste. Forcing manufacturers to use more expensive, or more easily biodegradable materials, or forcing them to pay refunds on cans or bottles, which will serve to provide future generations with more land and sea, raises the costs of production and increases the price of drinks and food. It boils down to a choice between the well being of this or future generations. It should at the same time be appreciated that future generations inherit more than our waste; they also receive all our valuable income-producing and consumption-satisfying assets.

2) *On safety and health*
Either the shareholder perhaps ultimately the consumer, or

6

maybe the taxpayer, will have to pay for the comprehensive tests of new products that may be demanded before they come to market. Safer drugs and also safer cars, trains, roads, airports and working environments, while undeniably of benefit, invariably cost more and may not be worth paying for. We could be safer on our way to and from, as well as at work, yet not earn enough to wish to cover the higher transport costs. In other words, we prefer to choose to take a chance with our lives on the road or in the sky. It is not coincidental that the safety of a country's transportation system is roughly in proportion to its average income. The better off you are, the more you will be inclined to pay for safety because the more you have to lose from an accident.

You, or somebody else, that is society at large, may be unwilling, or unable to pick up the bill for medical care that would save someone who is very dear, but, by definition, not dear enough. Decisions to turn off the life support systems have to be made all the time, in and out of hospital. They represent a very severe form of response to economic realities. It is one of the more important benefits of a higher income that, the better off you are, the longer you are likely to live. Rich people live longer, partly because they can afford more intensive care. Indeed one of the incentives to get rich is to be able to afford better care, so as to live longer and better.

A question that economists think worth asking is, how much in fact does it cost to save an extra life through a particular life-saving programme? The answer to this question will indicate which programmes are worth pursuing, in order to save as many lives as you are able to afford. It is a method known broadly as *cost–benefit* analysis. It encourages a form of competition for scarce resources, of which those promoting particular forms of life-saving expenditure programmes are, typically, not in favour. They would prefer to rely on the notion that life itself is priceless. The economist can still agree with the all-importance of life itself, but may also point out that a billion spent this way may be able to save many more lives than a billion spent some other way. For example, with the knowledge we have about the dangers of exposure to asbestos in buildings and what we know about the cost of removing asbestos from buildings, or substituting other materials with the same insulating, or fire protection properties, it is possible to calculate what each life saved by removing asbestos from buildings, actually costs. The numbers, in the case of the campaign against asbestos in US school buildings, are in fact very high – perhaps well into the billions of dollars per life saved. Thus, there would have been many more, (but different) lives saved, if the same resources, used to make for healthier school buildings, had been used in other ways.

The issue of how best to save lives is of course enormously complicated by the fact that the parents who send their kids to school are not paying for the improved buildings themselves. The improvement comes as a gift from taxpayers. Not that any savings made through not pursuing the clean-up would be likely to go to teachers or to the schools. In this way, emotions tend to take over from the economist's cost–benefit calculations.

3) *On paying wages, interest and insurance*
Another harsh fact of economic life is that proclaiming higher minimum rewards, or better working conditions for workers, will inevitably mean fewer employment opportunities for them. This is because less potential workers will be able to contribute sufficiently to the output of the firm to cover the costs of hiring them. The emphasis here on *rewards* from employment rather than wages is because the other employment benefits, including medical insurance, or pension contributions, which have become so important a feature of the employment contract, are not a gift of employers, even when they are forced, by law, to provide them. The cost could be to the account of the workers who keep their jobs, but take home less pay than they would otherwise do, because the employer is making contributions on their behalf for retirement, or insurance. Many workers, if they were free to choose from a menu of employment benefits, while recognizing their true cost, might prefer to take home more in cash and less in kind – or in other words, employment benefits. The extra costs of employing a worker may be recovered from customers in the form of higher prices. But these higher prices will mean less sales, output and employment and more demand for substitute goods from producers less encumbered by regulation of their employment conditions, or by taxes, or controls generally. Even if the regulations apply equally to all producers, which is unlikely, the alternative supplies may come from other countries

where firms are less burdened by both wages and regulated employment benefits.

All lenders need to be aware that the promise of higher returns for their savings from one, rather than another borrower, always implies higher risks to the lender. Of course, when the higher rewards prove illusory and there is every danger of lenders losing their savings, they may be able to call on the government, that is, the tax payer, or alternatively shareholders of, or depositors with, sound financial institutions to bail them out. But such actions will have their own consequences. The state may secure savers against default by financial institutions. If so, the responsibility for evaluating the risks that the banks or other financial institutions take, will have been transferred from the savers to its own officials. This will make banks and others so covered by government guarantees, inclined to take on more risky loans, if permitted to do so. Since the risks they take will not reduce their supply of funds, the costs of risk-taking are reduced, while the rewards remain as attractive as before. The result is more risk-taking and less reward for it, which is by no means desirable for society at large.

Another, perhaps uncomfortable fact of economic life, is that the less comfort or security potential borrowers are able to offer, the more expensive they will find it to raise credit, if indeed they are able to do so at all. Small businesses and poorer people are worse credit risks than large firms or richer people, for good reason. Their failure rates are much higher. And if banks are forced to deny the credit records of potential borrowers and this leads to a greater rate of default, the cost of supplying loans will generally rise and the demand for, and supply of, loans from credit-worthy borrowers will fall.

Similarly, eliminating the element of fault in medical, or any other kind of insurance, will lead people to visit their doctors more often and look after their cars and perhaps themselves less carefully. If crime pays better, because punishments become less harsh, or fewer crimes are solved, more crime will occur. If potential criminals have less to lose, in the form of better paid jobs, or even better social security, crime will seem a more attractive alternative and their victims will suffer accordingly.

If deposits are insured, the careful bankers lose out – as do careful drivers and parents when insurance goes "no fault" and the premiums bear no relation to the record of claims, or visits to the doctor or hospital.

Urban redevelopment, while perhaps improving the look of a town, by no means suits those who choose to pay low rents in run-down tenements, perhaps so they can be close to their work. Closing down a factory causes job losses, while it cleans the air and improves land values. Making it more difficult to dismiss workers, or managers, discourages firms from hiring them in the first instance. If established workers gain a higher degree of job security, potential workers find it harder to break in. Save the whale, nuke the whaler. Improve the air, condemn the Brazilian peasant to starvation. Fight AIDS, advance Cancer.

These are just a few examples of the absence of a free lunch – or of the lunch others are paying for. In general, abstract terms, the cost of any economic benefit supplied is the alternative "good" that might have been produced with the same inputs, that is, the same costs. Economists use the term *opportunity costs* to describe the true nature of costs. The cost is the other, useful, or next-best opportunity foregone, when a particular course of action is chosen. The cost is what else might have been achieved with the same resources, or, if it is leisure that is being consumed, in the same time. It is the particular task of economists to measure costs and to get others to recognize them.

Some Political Economy

When governments intervene in the economy, they may pretend that they are able to do so without serious consequences. It may even be argued that, in addition to merely making the world a kinder, gentler place, they will also make the economy more efficient. But every such interference, even when it is designed to replace, or supplement, some previous intervention by government, will inevitably promote some interests at the expense of others.

The tactic of those promoting some special interest is to cite the obvious lack of, and desperate need for, more or better of this or that. How often do we hear the earnest cry that something is wrong with us; that as a society we should be able to pay a living – that is higher wages – in more secure jobs; be more productive; design better; invent more; import less; export more; spend more on education of one kind or another; or on this or that research; produce superior art, or music, or literature; invest more; save more; waste less; protect nature; defend the accused in court; pay teachers more; employ more women or blacks and so on? If only we were more intelligent about it, we could have it all is the cry – and organized ourselves better, and paid heed to this or that prophet. What is seldom emphasized, is the sacrifices that these benefits necessarily entail. It is also not usually recognized that not all of us have the ability to become superstars in economic life any more than we have in athletics. Exactly why we cannot work more accurately and enthusiastically, sell harder, be more creative, get on better with our fellow workers, manage their and our own time better, invest more wisely, negotiate more astutely, as the best seem able to do, is seldom obvious.

The political game, of course, is to get more of what is good for us, and get others, less organized or persuasive, to pay for it. There was a time, at least until the 1960s, when economists were inclined to view the state as disinterestedly serving some purpose about which there was general agreement. Or, as economists were wont to put it grandly, well-meaning governments and the servants of the people, advised naturally by a cadre of disinterested economists, were to aim at a well-defined *social welfare function*, about which all would be in agreement. Private welfare could, it was thought, be *traded off* for social welfare, in a way that would make everybody better off.

The understanding most economists now have of the role of government is very different from the *public interest* view of it described above.[2] It is widely recognized that the state serves many different and often conflicting interests and politicians succeed by somehow satisfying, or reconciling, these interests better than their rivals. The state gives to some and takes away from others, without their consent, because it is a politically popular or acceptable action to take.

Private exchanges satisfy what is known as the *unanimity rule*. Both parties must agree and feel themselves better off for the deal struck or at least no worse off, or the exchange will not take place. All parties to the transaction have the right of veto. Governments would be able to do very little if every voter, like every buyer or seller, had the same right of veto. Only then, as with decisions of the UN Security Council, could we be sure that everybody was in agreement with every action taken. Satisfying 51 per cent of the voters may leave out a large number of very unhappy people. Also, of course, except in referendums, we do not vote yes or no, but for the package of policies provided by one party rather than another. Or perhaps one packager rather than another. We would certainly get less government if the voting rules required something much closer to unanimous agreement. Requiring 66 per cent, or more, of the elected representatives to agree to a change, makes it a lot more difficult to change a constitution.

It is also appreciated by the modern economist that the people who work for government are not, typically, very different in character to the rest of us. They, too, have their own welfare closest to their hearts. Also, it can be as much in their interests,as it would be for workers in any other kind of business, to be inventive in finding new work for themselves and their departments to do. The differences between the behaviour of people who work in the private and public sector, lies less in their character and qualifications, and much more in the nature of the checks and balances that convert the pursuit of private objectives into a public benefit. Businesses and their managers and workers have to pass the market test to survive. They compete with all other firms to give value to their customers. If they truly love to serve, it is because they have been especially blessed by training and temperament. Governments succeed by passing the electoral popularity test. Their officials succeed largely by impressing their superiors.

It should also be appreciated that it is politicians, in competition with one another, who determine the extent of the market, that is, the extent to which the economic outcomes are decided by a process of exchanges of resources and finished goods and services. And so businesses not only compete with one another, they compete in the political arena for freedom to operate and to restrict the freedom of other businesses to compete with them. Businesses, like all individuals, interest groups and parties, not only play by the rules; they also have opportunities to make them.

Politics versus the Economy

The problem for those who would resist the propaganda for change – who defend the status quo against initiatives of one kind or another – is that the benefits and beneficiaries of a particular policy intervention, are usually highly visible. The more is easily identified, while the less, that is to say the costs of the action, are typically spread widely. Who is actually paying and how much, cannot be easily isolated and identified among all the other contemporaneous forces influencing the economic outcomes.

For example, every import duty, or quota, or export subsidy, will be of conspicuous benefit to some firms and their employees. Removing, or reducing, the duty or subsidy can threaten not only a plant, but whole communities with disruption. The argument that consumers, or taxpayers generally, may have to pay more to save the day or that, by supporting some industries or firms, you are penalizing all others by raising their taxes and costs, may not be influential. The tax increases may, in themselves, be quite unimportant and it is seldom appreciated that total costs are made up of a large number of small items. The political victories of environmentalists over foresters will make homes more expensive – but who can say by how much? – and anyway, bricks can be substituted for wood and loggers can be retrained as bricklayers. Victory goes to the spotted owl. Enforcing the employment of under-represented groups is very likely to raise the costs of production to the disadvantage of poor consumers, who are likely to be more interested in the price they pay than in the race of the person who serves them. If it was not expected to raise costs, self-interested employers would have made the changes in hiring practices without the compulsion to do so.

Racial and sexual patterns of employment have undergone significant changes over time, as employers have sought out and
experimented with non-established labor that promised the
opportunity of lowering their costs. The inducement for the firm
to experiment, is the possibility of paying less than the established rate for the job. Less obviously, hiring non-traditional
labor is a method of avoiding an increase in the rate for the job,
when the competition from other employers for established labor
or traditional recruits is intensifying. That is why forcing firms to
pay the rate for the job – equal pay for equal work – which has
such a fair-minded ring to it, is an exclusive device. It discourages the firm from experimenting with the composition of the
labor force – experiments that are seldom very comfortable
exercises, especially in heterogeneous societies. It protects established labor – whites, men, union members – against their largely unproven potential competitors, who are willing to do the job
because they are able to earn more that way than in other
employment. Is it not fair to give them this opportunity to
improve themselves?

It is very difficult to convince women, or any other group, that
the reason firms have not employed more of them in more senior
positions is not prejudice or so-called *glass ceilings* that nobody
can see, but the result of a considered judgment of the costs and
benefits of doing so. It is no simple task to calculate the costs of
and the identity of who pays for the employment quotas. Also,
employers will naturally attempt to minimize these by employing
the best qualified and most advantaged of those officially defined
as disadvantaged. In practice, they may have been anything but
disadvantaged, except by their colour or religion and come from
very good homes, with wealthy parents, who sent them to the
best schools. Employers generally, when faced with this kind of
pressure, may tend to rely less on labor and more on machines,
to the great disadvantage of the unskilled and inexperienced
potential workers.

Changes that are forced upon firms by the state, are unlikely to
have any major impact that consumers, in general, will recognize
and, as a group, resist. Consumers are very hard to organize,
because there is not usually sufficient provocation in any one
measure to bring them to the barricades. Threatened producers

are much more focused. They are well informed, because a great deal is often at stake for them in a lower tariff, or a new tax, or a new financing scheme. And because so much is at stake, they are often able to attract sympathy from only marginally prejudiced outsiders. The latter must agree that it is not too much to ask them to pay more for foie gras so that patriotic French, rather than Italian geese may suffer on their behalf. In other words, they must feel better for their action, and perhaps be willing to ask others to make a small sacrifice as well.

The danger from all these individually impressive appeals for sympathy is that, if they are all given support, they will drag the economy down. If the economy is to grow, resources have to be redirected from declining industries to expanding ones and those that can stand on their own feet. This process may be painful to many in the established industries. But "no pain no gain" and somebody, after all, has to pay the taxes that cover the costs of protection. That "somebody" is, most conveniently, the growing firms and industries and their suppliers of all kinds.

Some overriding constitutional protection, or protection by way of free trading agreements with other countries, may be necessary to defend the principle of a competitive economy – to allow some firms and industries industries to fade away, so that others can grow. Defending the case for competition and efficiency against each particular piece of special pleading seeking protection, or subsidy, may be impossible. The emotions surrounding particular hardships are likely to win the political arguments. The future benefits to be derived from the growing firms are harder to recognize.

The recognition that imports have to be tolerated, so that your own industries are allowed to export, can avoid the political danger of having to treat each case for protection or subsidy on its own merits. The General Agreement on Tariffs and Trade (GATT),[3] as well as the North American Free Trade Agreement (NAFTA) and the European Union, are successful political devices that support the general interest in freer trade against the individual attacks on it. The principle of freer trade, if not always the detailed practice, can be politically popular. Moreover, exposure to international trade, forces the country to be conscious of the impact of any policy initiative (perhaps highly attractive when seen on its own), on the ability of its firms to compete internationally.

But protectionism can take forms other than high tariffs, or quotas for imports. It can be disguised in the form of environmental standards; or by the developed countries requiring employment practices, which low income countries may find very difficult to meet if they wish to remain competitive with higher-wage, but more productive, labor in the developed economies. There is the danger that low wages, which are the major competitive advantage held by low-income – and so low-wage – economies, may themselves be defined as an unfair trading practice by the officials in developed countries making the rules for "fair" trade. Also, low wage labor can be made much more expensive if the employer firms are forced to provide working conditions that are standard in developed economies.

Safer and more hygienic places of work, shorter working days, weeks and years, as well as hugely improved pay, all emerged in developing countries largely out of competition for workers who had become more productive. Workers, in effect, have traded better working conditions and fewer hours for less take-home pay. Employers competing with each other for labor, could not resist such demands for fear of losing their best workers. If regulation forces higher standards on the market, employment will be sacrificed for them. Employers will be unable to recover the extra costs of hiring some workers, usually the least productive of the work force, and they will be laid off, or fail to find employment. Legislating, or demanding better working conditions, is another way of imposing higher minimum wages, both within, and through fair trading policies beyond, the boundaries of the country. The frustrated workers would have been willing, if offered the choice, to work for less than the minimum wage, or in less than the minimum working environment. The workers who fail to gain employment because of artificially high minimum wages, or artificially favourable working conditions, are another politically impotent minority, prevented from competing as best they can with the majority.

Another potential area for abuse is the fair trading laws against *dumping*. Firms technically dump when the goods they produce are sold for less in the foreign market than in the domestic. Firms, typically, charge different prices in different markets, depending on the competition. They are what economists describe as *price discriminators*. The distinction between fair price discrimination and unfair cross subsidization is very difficult to make. In practice, firms may be regarded as dumping if they fail to earn what is defined as an adequate return on the investment they have made, or if they receive unfair advantages from their own governments. This could be by way of direct subsidies or – the same thing – low taxes. Deciding exactly what constitutes a level trading field, provides enormous scope for official discretion to protect domestic industries against competition, which is conveniently defined as dumping.

Given the limits imposed by a less than bounteous nature, and the enormous scope for some to stand in the way of income-enhancing transactions undertaken willingly by others; given also the opportunities which exist for politicians to protect some producers and to impose extra burdens on others; and given the political incentives to sacrifice long-term benefits for short-term advantages, it is perhaps a wonder that economies and average incomes have advanced in the way they have. It is to the economic success stories that we now turn.

1. This approach to what economists call externalities, originates with Ronald Coase of the University of Chicago. See R.H.Coase, *The Firm, the Market and the Law,* Chicago, University of Chicago Press, 1988.
2. The school of thought that developed this approach is known as the Public Choice School, of which American political economists Gordon Tullock and James Buchanan are regarded as the founders. For some further reading see Gordon Tullock, *Wealth, Poverty and Politics,* New York, Basil Blackwell, 1988 and James Buchanan, *Liberty, Market, and State: political economy in the 1980's,* New York, New York University Press, 1985.
3. To be renamed the World Trade Organisation (WTO) in January 1995.

CHAPTER TWO

BREAKING OUT

Overcoming the niggardliness of nature. Getting it more or less right

S ince time immemorial most individuals and societies have struggled desperately and vainly against nature. With rare exceptions, survival demanded an unremitting struggle and any surplus was a temporary gift of nature, which some other powerful party was likely to take away. Yet, as we are all aware, this is not the experience of large numbers of people today. An unprecedentedly numerous (and still growing) group of men and women, concentrated mostly in a group of countries described as *developed* or industrialized, now experience a standard of living, a command over goods or, perhaps more correctly, nature, that could not have been dreamed of 200 or even 100 years ago. A state of affairs where, as we are informed, the main dietary threat to health is not starvation but that of eating too much of the wrong kind of food. Their relative inexperience with a state of material abundance produces its own stresses, but hunger and exposure to cold and epidemics are human tragedies remote from the direct experience of almost all the citizens of the developed economies.

The importance of ideas

How then did this great explosion of consumption power come about? How did so many people become so much more productive and so escape the poverty that has long trapped and still burdens so many around the world? What are their lessons from this experience, both for the citizens of countries who mostly enjoy the advantages of a good standard of living and others who would wish to join them in this? Is there any limit to what may be produced and consumed by individuals or groups? Since history provides us with examples of economic retrogression, as well as of progress, what are the factors that will not only prevent economic growth but cause economies to shrink? Present well-being should surely not be taken for granted. These are fundamental questions for which we can hope to find some answers.

All economic progress – the process of getting more value out of the resources put into production – starts with an idea. Ideas include those about new, or better products, or ways of promoting or producing them; using alternative materials or methods; motivating workers better; making superior financing arrangements; establishing more favourable locations. All these, among other innovations, may help to promote a more favourable relationship between the cost of the inputs and the value of the final product.

The farmer imagines a better way to plough his fields, or more suitable crops to grow on them and experiments successfully with these new methods. Other farmers follow suit. An engineer satisfies himself and persuades an architect who convinces a property developer, that by using steel and concrete they can raise more stories than any bricklayer. Developing this idea makes land in the city centre more productive, as it comes to support more economic activity and so produces more rental income. Another practical man imagines the advantages of the internal combustion engine over horse power and gets the opportunity to prove it. Having travelled the first mile with steam power, other men decide to build further on the original concept and huge gains over nature are made. The coal, when added to the steam boiler, adds much more value than it did when keeping the home fires burning. And so the demand for coal increases.

19

But so also does the supply of coal, as improved and lower-cost methods for mining coal are applied with increasing success.

The factory and shop floors can be highly fertile ground for improved methods. New ideas that increase the value of productive resources are generated wherever people are encouraged to think about their work. Creativity is not confined to art studios, or advertising agencies. Accountants, not to mention bankers and financiers, can thrive on successful innovations that reduce the cost of an audit or better suit the requirements of borrowers and lenders, so reducing the cost of attracting savings to particular uses.

The key to economic progress is improved knowledge of the behaviour of both nature and man, and in the practical application of such knowledge. Some ideas have been more important in solving economic problems than others. But to describe the process of discovery and application that has given man so much more economic power, is not to explain why or when it happened, and why it continues to force the changes that make us, and others, so much more productive. After all, though he is often better fed and sheltered than his ancestors, and therefore more able to apply his mind, man does not obviously have more brain power than they had. What then has made the difference?

Taking the gap. The essence of realizing change for the better

The key factor stimulating new ideas that lead to new methods, and new products that add value, by improving the ratio between the cost of the inputs and the value of the outputs, is the opportunity and the incentive to innovate. The degree of encouragement which individuals receive, to challenge established methods and products with something new or better, is surely the crucial ingredient for economic progress. The potential improvements in productive power that begin with an idea, can only be realized if the originators of new ideas are allowed the opportunity to innovate and experiment; that is, to exercise what economists think of as their *entrepreneurial* powers. Anything may be possible physically, but the experiments with change have to be encouraged in order to challenge established thoughts, methods, materials, organizations and even organizational forms themselves. Change has to be welcomed and the entrepreneurs have to be confident that they will be appropriately rewarded should their plans come together..

If there is value added, then the surplus could go to the innovating individual or enterprise. It could be shared with the workers, or managers, or with the broader community, by way of taxes on the extra income. It seems obvious that the more the innovators are able to keep for themselves, the greater the inducement to further innovation and enterprise. Also, the more they stand to lose in taxes or other levies, the more cautious they are likely to be. These are but the generalities that the economist relies upon. How much incentive will be enough in every instance is not clear and adequate reward may, of course, be derived in other than an obviously material form.

Competition from new methods of producing, and, perhaps more important, the process that makes previously unknown finished goods, services and materials available for potential users to choose from, are the essential features of materially progressive societies. It is the application of new ideas that has transformed the physical character of the modern house, office and factory over the past 100 years.

The potential reward for innovation, for introducing any new good or method, is to create, or widen the gap between what others are willing to pay for the good or service and what it costs to produce. Innovation forces open that gap. That is how the system gets more out of what is put in and adds value. The gap opens up because some people prove that they can get more out of the inputs (which may include their own time) that go into the process of production than can others. The risk in this process is that the entrepreneur will be proved wrong, and if so, resources will have been wasted and value lost in the process.

Adding value and sharing in it

The entrepreneur utilizes inputs of labour, land and capital, as well as goods and services produced by others, for which, naturally, a market-related price has to be paid. That price, or hiring charge, is based on what the inputs are expected to contribute elsewhere – their opportunity cost. Value is added by using the same inputs to produce something that society judges to be worth more. The value, that is, the price of the new product or service – like the old is established in the market place, by the reaction of buyers to available supplies.

The gap between price and cost might also be closed through regulation when the full consequences of an innovation are revealed. Regulation may force increases in costs of production, making it less attractive to supply. Also taxes, or worse, outright prohibitions, may be imposed, with the intention of restricting demand, or eliminating it altogether. So-called sumptuary taxes on tobacco or alcohol are commonplace, as are restrictions on demands for foreign exchange, or foreign labour or goods. Restrictions on hiring workers with the wrong skin colour or religion, are a way of restricting the competition offered by these groups. Restricting the demand for land, buildings, or rented accommodation to buyers or hirers with the right racial or religious qualifications, serves the same purpose.

Closing the gap

Any gap created, any proven surplus from any new product, method or material, when retained by the entrepreneur or the enterprise, will set up a chain of reactions. The innovating firm will want to expand to produce more of the profitable item, or use more of the helpful material or method. Other producers will want to follow, unless the innovator is protected by patents or licenses, or by monopoly rights issued by the government. In this way, extra supplies of the more valuable product or service will be forthcoming, as will extra demands for an improved material or method. Extra demand, or extra supply, will tend to close the gap between cost and price. The advantage will be transferred, gradually, from the innovating producers to their customers and the value of the idea falls away as prices again come to approximate the full costs of production. This process, of action and reaction to the gap between price and cost, is as continuous as the flow of new ideas and the attempts to implement them. In this way, the self-interested exploitation of any perceived margin between price and cost, works to eliminate it and so promotes, quite unintentionally, the public interest, in an ever wider menu of opportunities to buy or sell on the best possible terms. Adam Smith, in 1786, described these helpful, unintended consequences of self-interested behaviour as the *hidden hand*.

The rewards for superior technique and the role of competition for resources

As has been emphasized, innovations expand the gap between price and cost to the advantage of the entrepreneur or inventor and society at large. These ideas shake resources out of previous uses. At any moment, there are always some marginal suppliers who, given the price buyers prove willing to pay, do no more than cover their costs. Any increase in costs or reduction in prices, as the result of an innovation anywhere in the economy, which results in a shift in demand or supply away from the previous pattern, will force these suppliers out of that particular activity. The market prices of all well-established products or services will therefore approximate the costs of the most vulnerable of them – the marginal producers. Those who are able to supply at less than these costs make a profit, that is, in the economists' sense of that term, when the value of their output is in excess of the opportunity cost of the resources they use up in the process.

Successful enterprises are encouraged to grow, to take advantage of the gap that they have opened up. They grow by competing away scarce resources from less capable firms and by generating more value from them. In this way, through encouraging competition for resources and the survival of the competent, society can ensure that scarce resources are being well used.

In the next chapter we will introduce further thoughts about competition – how it works and how it may be inhibited in practice.

23

CHAPTER THREE

UNDERSTANDING COMPETITION

How big is too big?

The most important form of competition that protects the interests of buyers against sellers, is probably that between the new and the old, rather than between established producers of the familiar. The producers of beer do not only compete with each other, or with the manufacturers, producers and marketers of cider, wine, soft drinks or other alcoholic drinks. They also compete with every imaginable as well as presently unimaginable way in which their potential customers can dispose of their time and money.

Competition policy has focused on the structure of established industries, or sectors, with the presumption that the smaller the market share of the largest producers, the more desirably competitive will be conditions in that industry or sector of the economy. Such concerns can lead to the prevention of mergers and acquisitions, or even to the break-up of, or restrictions on, the growth of profitable firms in a particular sector of the economy, when they threaten to get too big. "Too big" means that they dominate their markets. [1]

Such interventions can have highly perverse results. They may in fact prevent the more efficient producers from growing, in order to protect their smaller, less efficient rivals. So consumers may end up paying more for inferior goods and services, in return for the appearance of more competition. These restrictions can prevent the true competitive outcome, which could mean few firms, or even one dominating an industry. If all the available economies of larger scale are to be realized, there may be room, particularly in a small national economy, for only one, or perhaps two, internationally competitive producers. For example, even the largest economies are incapable of absorbing the full output of more than, at most, a few aluminum smelters, if they are to operate at the lowest cost per unit of output. For smaller economies, there may be room for only one internationally competitive oil refinery or cement plant. Clearly it would make no economic sense to insist on breaking up such a producer into a number of separate, high-cost firms, on the principle that more is better than few.

An obvious solution to such problems is to open the domestic market to competition from producers in other countries. By redefining the market in this way, to mean the whole wide world, there will almost always be rivals for even the largest firms. It is not coincidental that so called anti-trust actions against large dominant firms have been taken furthest in the USA. The USA is the largest economy by far whose reliance on international trade was at one time comparatively limited. It was natural, given the great economic progress made in the USA by comparison with the rest of the world, for the politicians there to worry less about economic efficiency and more about populist resentment of large-scale enterprise and the social excesses of their owners and controllers. More recently, as the world economy and US dependence on trade with it has grown more important, and as the economic rivalry of other countries has become more impressive and threatening to US dominance, the view that regulating the size and behaviour of large corporations by means of anti-trust policies might well inhibit the ability of the USA to compete globally, is receiving much more critical attention.

The problem for the authorities, in assessing the appropriate structure of firms or industries, is that it is impossible to determine how big or dominant a firm might be if left to its own devices. The answer can only be found in the market place itself – in the attempts firms make to take advantage of the expected gap between prices and costs and to expand the firm and its share of the market accordingly. The margin between price and cost may widen, and yet prices can decline if costs decline more rapidly than the prices realized by an expanding enterprise. Lower prices are the means which firms may use to increase the size of their markets. And the larger market, or market share, gives them opportunities to realize production economies of size. Thus a firm may become dominant in its market and therefore much more profitable by reducing prices and costs. A Monopoly may be the result of a competitive process from which consumers would benefit. The best response of government to such possibilities would be to leave such decisions about growth to the firms themselves, and not to concern themselves with the potential abuse of monopoly powers.

Moreover, concern for market share in particular industries comes from far too narrow an understanding of the nature of the market and competition in it. The market is as wide as you want to define it, territorially. It could be the street, the suburb, the town, country or the whole wide world. The smaller the territory, the greater the degree of monopoly power. One would not insist on a brewery on every street corner, because beer would be too expensive that way. The competitive outcome may well be one beer producer in a town, or even a country. The beer drinkers, however, will be well protected by the potential entry of other producers, should the successful local or regional brewer rest on its laurels and attempt to exploit rather than grow the beer market. Beer will also be imported. Furthermore, competition between beer producers is not particularly important anyway, since there are many substitutes for beer, of which the brewer will be aware, and this will determine his behaviour.

European countries, especially Germany and the UK,

conscious that their companies were competing in world markets, and in particular with firms in the USA, had little political difficulty in tolerating the growth of very large firms, or in allowing mergers and cartels for the purpose of achieving efficient production for world markets on a large scale. It is not at all clear that consumers were disadvantaged by the authorities turning a blind eye to huge size, or cartels, unless perhaps these large firms were able to discriminate against their domestic customers. This is only possible when the domestic firms are protected against imports.

Providing protection against imports has been used as a strategy by governments intent on picking winning industries. Profits from a protected local market would then be required to be reinvested, with the aim of growing the firms in order to allow them to compete effectively with the world's best. In these cases, the government is taxing consumers in order to finance its gamble on what it hopes will be a winning industry.

The developer of an entirely new product or service will always enjoy a degree of monopoly power – that is to say benefit – from what is new or different. Inevitably however, there will be closer or more distant substitutes for the new good in question and certain producers will be more directly threatened by an innovation than others. Governments recognize such rights by registering patents, trademarks and copyrights that secure the inventor against other parties copying their creation. Clearly, consumers would benefit in the short run if others were allowed to compete in this way. Generic drugs, as opposed to proprietary, are cheaper because their prices need only cover their direct costs of production, which do not include the costs of research and development, or of promoting the new remedy.

But such copies are permitted only when the patents run out. Governments protect intellectual property in order to encourage invention. Without such protection, there would be little material incentive to invent a new drug, or write a book, or compose music. Society protects physical property against seizure or theft for similar practical reasons, and that is to encourage savings and wealth creation. Intellectual property gets the special protection of patents, trade marks and copyright, because it is harder to recognize the fruits of intellectual effort than of savings that find their form in physical assets, plant and equipment, or financial claims on them.

The case against policies that restrict the market share of the largest producers is similar to the case for patents. That is, there are always more or fewer close substitutes and the drive for new and better use of resources should not be inhibited.

Policies against competition

In practice, competition policies, especially in the USA, have often been used to protect the less efficient firms against the competition of a powerful rival. The argument is often and easily made, that the dominant firm has gained, or maintained, a large share of the market through the use of some unfair business practice, rather than because it has proved itself a superior servant of its customers. Almost by definition, being successful means making trading conditions difficult for rivals. The courts, rather than the customers, get to decide the market outcomes in disputes of this kind. It is also nice work for the economists, who get the opportunity to display their powers of reason before a learned judge, even though their ability to offer conclusive advice as to why firms do it this way rather than that, is limited. It is all too easy for the courts to confuse an appearance of competition – the existence of many producers of like products – with the end result of competition. The result may well be highly satisfied customers, who are well served by a few firms, or perhaps only one.

An argument against leaving well alone, is that we cannot be sure that the dominant firm will continue to give the good service that first gave it such a strong position. The rejoinder to this, is that there is indeed no certainty that the firm will continue to perform for consumers as well in the future as it has in the past. On the other hand it may. Given all this uncertainty therefore, is it not best to rely on the competition from firms that provide close substitutes, as well as on the development of new technology that may bring new entrants into the market? Such entrants could very easily emerge from the ranks of disaffected managers of a once all-powerful firm. They are well placed to take advantage of any emerging complacency or incompetence or disregard for their customers.

There are in fact some quite simple tests to discover whether profits are the result of competition or the rewards for inhibiting competition. If the profitable firm, or firms, are in fact expanding their markets then, by definition, competitive forces are at work. If the markets are stagnant and the firms remain highly profitable, then a closer look is called for to discover why the profits are not enticing additional output, or the entry of competitors into the market. Almost inevitably it will be found that, if there are barriers to entry, or to increasing output, the government itself will be responsible for the restrictions, for reasons that make political sense, but are clearly not helpful to consumers.

Tariffs, or quotas against imports, may be a source of protection. Strategic concerns, or plans, may also protect the local producers. They may be guaranteed a return on their investments sufficient to keep them in business, at least until the next war. This, in turn, can mean higher controlled or regulated prices which the consumer is forced to pay, with the government making sure that nobody breaks ranks. Limiting entry into any industry or service, including the professions, by the award of licenses, is another obvious way to restrict entry and competition. Compulsory single channel marketing schemes for agricultural products are designed to prevent farmers from competing with each other. All these restrictions make for the most secure form of monopoly power – that sanctioned by the government itself.

Main street banks in the USA reacted to the threat of larger banks by preventing the evolution of branch banking networks throughout the country. Large banks, with many branches, have dominated banking systems almost everywhere else, because they are more efficient. Populist resentment of economic power also prevented strategic alliances developing in the USA between financial houses and operating companies, that are so important (and welcome) a feature of business almost everywhere else. Such alliances were very much a feature of the US economy until the 1930s, under the leadership of J.P. Morgan and others of his kind. The banking reforms known as the Glass–Steagal Act were directed against the Morgan Bank and forced the separation of commercial and investment banking, a separation that holds to this day. Simply put, deposit-taking banks in the USA are not allowed to hold shares. Many critics, including those economists thought of as on the left of the politico-economic spectrum, now think that the inability of US banks to form alliances with other companies, by way of providing them with both debt and equity capital, is one of the important explanations for the inability of US firms to compete successfully with their Japanese rivals.[2]

The economist's notion of an ideal world

Economic analysis has, in fact, little to say that is very precise about the benefits of a dynamic process of competitive action and reaction. The only precise judgments economists can make about the necessary conditions for the efficient use of scarce resources, apply to a fantasy world entirely of the economist's imaginings — the world of so-called *perfect competition*. This is a theoretical construct, in which everything about the economic future and the past is known. There is no ignorance or uncertainty about the future and so innovation is impossible. In this world there are no new products, or methods, or promotion of sales, or use of trade marks, or any proprietary knowledge which form such important features of the modern economy. This world, inhabited only by economists, is one without change, where all firms are small, all buyers are one of many, and neither buyers nor sellers have any influence on market prices. They are, as it is said, price takers rather than price makers. There are also no significant economies of scale. Thus the efficient, perfectly competitive firm, producing at lowest possible cost, is a small one with many rivals.

Given perfect competition, the least-cost outcome, where output is as large as the available inputs allow, is demonstrated to be where prices are equal to costs and costs are at a minimum. As far as resources are concerned, they earn rewards equal to the product of the last unit just worth employing. Therefore wages are equal to the product of the marginal worker, the last worker worth employing. Interest is equal to the product of the last unit of capital worth employing and the rent paid for land is equal to the output of the last unit of land worth cultivating. Since there is nothing unknown, there are no risks and no economic profits – that is to say no gap between prices and costs, including the cost of capital. The providers of capital earn only a *normal return*. This is the economist's ideal world.

Clearly all discussions have to start somewhere and it is no criticism of a theoretical construct to say that it is unrealistic. All theories are simplifications. They are judged by what comes out of the theory – predictions, rather than assumptions. Also helpful is to relax the assumptions and see if the predictions of the original theory still hold. The perfect competition model can explain what will happen to prices should the harvest fail and no imports be possible. But such analysis has little to say about the optimal size or structure of the firm, or what may be economically efficient outcomes, maximizing output for available inputs in the real world, where people are inventing new products and methods and when the future is uncertain. Unfortunately, the notion that many producers in a defined sector of the economy are somehow better than fewer, because only then are producers unable to influence the price of their output, is a totally misleading conclusion drawn from the perfect competition model.

In the absence of any precise guidelines from economic analysis, competition policy becomes a matter of judgment and legal precedent. But such judgments are, as indicated, seldom without political consequence or interest. Popular feelings against the large and powerful, may have nothing to do with the efficiency with which the large firms or banks go about their business and their ability to meet the demands of the customers they serve. It may have much more to do with an atavistic resentment of success, which can be exploited by the smaller firms threatened by competition from the large firms, and which politicians must take seriously.

Opening and closing the gap – a modern case study

About 50 years ago the computer changed from a figment of the imagination of brilliant mathematicians, into an item only the most powerful of governments, and later, firms, could afford. For

20 or 30 years after that, what were very large calculating machines were supplied by a few firms, of whom IBM became the most important. IBM for many years sold its large and increasingly powerful mainframe computer systems for far more than they cost to produce. This was to the great advantage of IBM shareholders and managers and workers and also to that of their customers, who proved very willing to support IBM. But computers consistently became smaller, more powerful and cheaper to produce. The personal computer of 1980 was capable of more calculations and applications than the giant machines of 20 years before and were assembled where labour was relatively cheap. Many of the components that made up computers were mass-produced by firms around the world. Electric circuits that once filled whole rooms with expensive copper and steel, were printed on minute pieces of glass that were churned out in their billions by the most sophisticated of manufacturing methods, and to the most exacting standards. And so the prices of these small computers and more important, the cost of a standardized unit of computing power, fell dramatically, to a minute fraction of the cost 10 years before. Small computers and networks of them, have became as familiar as the typewriter in the office and home.

The gap between price and the costs of production of computers closed as their prices declined. The personal computer, and more so their components produced around the world, became commodities like steel or cotton, with very similar characteristics. These trends were greatly to the disadvantage of the giant IBM which had specialized in the production and distribution of large computers, now increasingly competing with smaller computers and their networks. In fact in 1992 IBM made the largest recorded loss in US economic history.

The most successful firms in the computer industry are now those writing operating instructions for computers. They are supplying a rapidly growing demand at prices that, for a few firms, handsomely cover their costs which are mainly salaries for writers of software. The importance of ideas is very obvious when the product is a minute disk made of cheap plastic.

In its great days, when it so dominated the computer market, IBM was called upon to defend its practices in a hugely expensive anti-trust action brought against it by the US government. After both sides had spent over 1 billion dollars on legal expenses the case was abandoned. It is no coincidence that the leading software house, Microsoft, now the dominant software producer, has been under investigation on a charge of unfair practices brought by its competitors. The charge seems to be, that it gives Microsoft an unfair advantage to sell the systems which enable both operation and application of the small computer. Recently, Microsoft reached a settlement with the US authorities, to allow competitors earlier access to its own computer operating systems technology. This will enable them to compete, so it is thought, more effectively with Microsoft, in writing applied software programmes that have to adapt to the new computer operating systems in which Microsoft has had so much success – first with Microsoft DOS (disk operating system), and more recently with Microsoft Windows technology, which has become the major gateway for all software applications.

Competition on the demand side

While it is possible to rank suppliers according to their ability to produce below full cost, including a charge for capital, it is also possible to rank the intensity with which goods or services are desired. Just as price tends to equal the costs of the least capable surviving producers, the same market price will be low enough to attract demand from the *marginal consumer*. That is, the preferences of the consumer at the margin, one largely indifferent to spending money and/or time on the particular good on offer, or something else. The actions of the just-surviving producer and the least intense consumers will be the decisive influence, at least in the short run, on the prices actually charged for and the quantities produced of, any particular good or service. There will be many consumers who would have paid more than the going price, but do not have to do so because of the incentives which producers have to expand sales by lowering prices, or improving service, in order to attract custom less keen than theirs. Similarly, the more efficient producers would be able to supply at prices lower than the prices required to keep part of the competition – the barely surviving producer – in business. They would still be able to cover their own lower costs at lower prices, but they clearly are more profitable charging no less than some of their less efficient competitors. However, they will have every incentive to reinvest their profits so as to expand their capacity to achieve a bigger and more profitable share of the market. It is this additional capacity that will tend to force down prices and force the previously marginal producer out of the industry.

The difference between what the *intra-marginal consumers* would have willingly paid, had the suppliers been able, in some practical way, to identify them among their other customers, and what they do pay, is what economists call their *consumer surplus*. This is why the wine afficionado pays no more for the most expensive item on the wine list than the parvenu salesman trying to impress a client. Similarly, the difference between this market price and the costs of producing the good or service, is called a *producer surplus* by economists.

We observe *price discrimination* when producers transfer consumer surplus from their customers to themselves, where it is economic to do so – in other words where the benefits in extra revenue cover the costs of segmenting the market. Thus, because of their easily identified age, pensioners and children pay less to go to the movies – and more of them attend – and fill up seats at off-peak times. Because their time is worth more, with the result that they tend to make shorter trips, business travellers can be identified by airlines and be made to pay more to travel than the tourist sitting next to them. The key to the practice of price discrimination is the ability of the carriers or theatre owners to prevent resale.

Lawyers and medical doctors also charge *what the traffic will bear*, in order to fill up their capacity. They tend to take leave of their less valuable clients when their increasingly valuable time is more fully engaged with those with the ability and willingness to pay more.

A supermarket would probably attract more custom if only it could organize the check-out lines according to the income of its customers, at a cost that was equal to, or less than, the extra benefits to customers. These could then charge a premium for quick service and provide a discount to those prepared to wait in line. The best supermarkets seem to be able to do, is to open more stores and more check-out points at peak times, and fewer at times when those with time on their hands typically shop. This is a case of a peak load problem which supermarkets clearly have more difficulty in solving than electric utilities, which vary the charge according to the time of day. By reducing demand at peak times by charging more then and increasing demand at other times, an electric or telephone company can manage with less capacity and so reduce its costs.

These examples of what is called price discrimination, describe one of the attempts that buyers and sellers make to solve their own economic problems. It would be very unwise to rule out price discrimination on principle because it is seen to help some and harm others. What is clear is that, if you prevented the airlines from charging the business traveller more and the backpacker less, fewer planes would fly. Again, competition between airlines, or between airlines and the makers of buses and motor cars, or between the producers of different sources of energy, to increase their sales, means that any economies, any margin over costs, will tend to reduce prices and/or improve quality, to the advantage of buyers generally.

1. The recent interest of the US Federal Trade Commission and the Department of Justice in the practices of what has become the pre-eminent computer software company, Microsoft, provides another case study of this kind. The previous interest of these government agencies in what was once the all-powerful producer of computers, IBM, is another.
2. See for example Lester C. Thurow, *Head to Head: The coming battle among Japan, Europe and America,* New York, Morrow, 1992.

CHAPTER FOUR

DIFFERENT WAYS OF SEEING THE ECONOMIC WORLD

Economists and Accountants on the Definition of Income

The profits measured by accountants differ from those of economists mostly in that, following tax law, they make a distinction between the cost of funds supplied by owners – equity or share capital – and funds borrowed from banks and others – the firm's debt finance. Such loans carry an interest charge which is deducted from operating profits for the purpose of calculating taxable income. No equivalent deduction, however, is allowed for the opportunity costs of equity finance, of utilizing your own savings in your own enterprise. Thus firms with more equity capital appear more profitable to accountants. They also pay more tax on higher levels of reported income. To the economist, scarce capital is scarce capital, irrespective of the contractual arrangements that link the suppliers of capital – the savers and lenders – to the users of capital – the investors and borrowers. For economists and rational economic actors, capital – that is to say accumulated savings – has a value in some alternative use, an opportunity cost. This cost, or opportunity foregone, is something that the individual or company using their own capital cannot ignore. The cost of capital may be explicit, in the form of interest paid on borrowed funds, or implicit as the returns that would be available to the saver/investor of scarce capital in alternative uses. The firm, accordingly, makes an economic, as opposed to an accounting profit, when it earns a return on all the capital employed in the firm that exceeds its opportunity cost. That is, gives a return over and above the return from an equivalent investment in some similar project managed by someone else.

The other main area for dispute between the economist, the accountant and the tax collector, is in the provision made for *capital consumption* or depreciation in the calculation of income. The economist's notion of depreciation is the loss of real value, or real consumption power, suffered by the owner of the machine over a period of time. Economic depreciation is equivalent to the change in the real value of the machine over time, which, in turn, is equal to changes in the market value of the used machine, adjusted for changes in the general level of prices. Another way of thinking about this, is to imagine the firm putting aside the amounts allowed for depreciation in a fund that would be sufficient to cover the purchase price of a new machine to replace the one that had worn out. If so, the owner of the machine would have been fully compensated for the capital losses arising out of ownership.

The problem for the accountant and the receiver of revenue, is that of finding a practical counterpart for economic depreciation for machines that have very different lives, or very specific uses that preclude a wide market for them. To call for a formal appraisal of the value of all machines used each year, while appropriate in principle, is clearly not a practical solution.

The actual allowances provided by the taxing authority for equipment and materials, which reduce taxable income and so taxes paid, have to be based on loose rules of thumb about economic depreciation. This provides great scope for manipulating the business tax system to favour particular kinds of investment, or investment generally, by allowing generous allowances for some sectors or purposes.

It is also possible for the tax authorities not to allow the investors enough for depreciation. This is particularly likely to happen when the rate of inflation is rising. In this case, any depreciation allowances, based upon the actual historical cost of the machines, will not be enough to provide for replacing them, should the firm wish to do so. The possibility that the firm will have to pay higher effective taxes on its income will discourage investment. For this and other reasons that rest heavily on a complicated definition of income, or rather on the classification of the expenditures of the business enterprise that are accepted as a deduction from income for the measurement of taxable income, nominal and effective business tax rates may differ widely. That is to say, taxes actually paid as a proportion of the extra consumption power the firm may have created for its owners, may differ from country to country and industry to industry, even from firm to firm, in the same industry.

An economist would define income as the amount of potential consumption power, generated by the firm or individual, over a period from all sources, from supplying labor, or savings, or real estate, or through directly owning assets which increase in market value ahead of inflation. These capital gains are a source of consumption power, whether realized or not. The problem for the tax authorities wishing, consistently, to tax real income from capital gains, is that the market value of such assets is only unambiguously established upon selling. But if only realized gains are to be taxed, then strong incentives will have been set up to avoid realization and little will be collected in taxes. Making proper allowance for inflation sets another practical problem in assessing capital gains as income.

The survival of the firm

If a firm is to survive over the long term it must earn, or rather be expected to earn, at least enough, after taxes, to cover its full opportunity costs or interest foregone – the cost of materials and labor time, the opportunity cost of savings applied in the enterprise. It must cover the interest, or dividend payments required by the suppliers of capital, as well as replace its equipment that will wear out over time. It will survive by being able to raise additional debt or equity capital, in competition with all other borrowers, to invest in replacement plant and equipment. The additional funds required may be obtained from the shareholders, in the form of cash retained rather than distributed to shareholders, or they may be provided by bankers and other lenders, or raised through additional share issues. The size of the firm is therefore limited by its ability to raise finance, and raising finance for expansion or the replacement of assets depends on the ability of the firm to cover its *cost of capital*.

If the firm fails to cover, or, more accurately, is not expected to cover, these full costs, it may survive for an extended period of time by merely covering its operating costs – that is, the cost of labor and materials used with the machines, until they wear out. Instead of disposing of its equipment and other physical capital, the firm may be allowed by its owners or bankers to use up its assets over time. Under these conditions the capital will not be worth replacing and the firm, like old soldiers, will simply fade away.

A firm may go bankrupt, that is be worthless to its shareholders, if it fails to meet its contractual obligations to pay interest, rent, taxes or wages and salaries. The physical assets of the firm will then be sold off to meet the debts of the company. These assets will have a value depending on the expected difference between the costs of operating them and the income generated. Again, only if the value in use is less than the scrap value, will a machine be abandoned to the scrap merchants.

As well as bankruptcy, takeovers and mergers are mechanisms for transferring the use of potentially valuable equipment from less to more competent managers. The competent managers may simply have greater skill in persuading banks, other lenders, or shareholders to provide them with capital on superior terms.

Clearly, managers and owners have incentives to avoid the costs of bankruptcy. They reduce the risks of bankruptcy by raising a greater proportion of their investment requirements in return for a share of profits, (equity capital) and by raising long- rather than short-term loans. Also, the more able they are to turn physical assets at short notice into cash, the less vulnerable they are to bankruptcy. So the more reliant the firm is on highly specialized equipment, the value of which is difficult to realize other than through use, the more exposed it will be to a cash crisis, that is, to bankruptcy. Fixed, or unavoidable costs add to the risks of bankruptcy. If output can be adapted very easily to variations in demand and most of the costs of the firm can be made to vary directly with output, the firm will be much better placed to survive the unexpected falls in demand that might otherwise threaten bankruptcy. Another concern of the firm will be the ease with which it is able to reduce the number of employees. If dismissal is only possible with significant redundancy payments, this will make the workforce much more like a fixed cost of production and by so doing, generally discourage employment, or at least permanent employment.

The accountants keep the records and judgments can be made about how well the firm has performed from the information they provide. The usual measures of performance are based upon the amount of money the owners of the firm invested as equity or risk capital. It is the ratio of income, more or less appropriately adjusted for taxation, to the owners' capital, that constitutes the measure of relative success or failure. Economists would modify this judgment to allow for the opportunity cost of this capital. That is to say, they adjust for what the capital could have been expected to earn from similar projects under different management. A profitable firm then earns a return in excess of this opportunity cost. They would also expect higher returns from projects that are riskier – and so more likely to fail.

Accountants, typically, measure the value of the capital employed in a firm, on the basis of investments made in moneys of the day over time. Economists regard what some item of equipment cost, or was worth at one point in time, as of historical interest only. What really matters is the market value of the asset today. This depends upon the value it is expected to add for its owners at present values. Bygones are bygones as far as members of society and economists are concerned. If an unwise investment decision was made in the past, that should not influence decisions in respect of those assets today. If their value, when sold, is worth more to the firm or owner than if held, the appropriate decision is to sell, even if that should mean having to record an accounting loss. The economic waste occurred long before that.

Homo economicus

The central presumption of economic analysis is that the actors under observation are economic men and women. That is to say, they simply prefer more goods of one kind to another and consistently or rationally pursue that preference. The presumption is that they will maximize or behave optimally, subject to the constraints of limited resources and knowledge. The assumption that economic actors have these consistent goals makes behaviour predictable, at least in principle, and allows economists to make their predictions. That is, it enables them to say, "If this happens, then that will follow". *If* prices rise *then,* then demand will fall, which is a prediction always made with the suitable qualification that everything else that might also influence demand, (for example incomes and tastes), is held to remain the same.

These qualifications play the role of the controlled experiments conducted in laboratories. The atmospheric pressure is held constant and so on. There are no one-handed economists, for the very good reason that more than one factor may be important in influencing outcomes – each equally likely. The only predictions economists are able to make are qualified ones.[1]

In practice, unravelling the full logic of the activities under observation, explaining why the particular practice – for example, the contracts signed between one or other party – in fact does make economic sense, is what stretches the imagination and skills of the economist. It is the attempts to explain what was

41

previously not understood, or to challenge what was provisional-
ly accepted as a good explanation, that fills the journals only
other economists read. The explanations offered are consistent
with the fundamental presumption that the phenomenon
observed represents optimizing behaviour, subject to unavoidable limits or constraints. The constraints may take the form of a
lack of knowledge or information, which, while potentially available, is regarded as too expensive to acquire.

The presumption of consistency or rationality goes further. All
economic actions have consequences over time. The plans are
made for tomorrow as well as today. Therefore economic man
has rational expectations, that is considered and consistent
thoughts and working hypotheses about the future consequences
of the actions which they and others take, based upon past experience. These expectations may not necessarily be fulfilled, the
plans may fail, but not, it should be assumed, because of stupidity or avoidable ignorance. They may fail because the future is
not always like the past, because of something new under the
sun. But whether it is bad luck or bad judgement, the planners
and their plans do not fail repeatedly because of the penalties for
failure. The unfit or the unlucky hostages to an uncertain future
will not pass the test of economic survival.

It is the presumption that people take well-informed decisions,
that on average they are doing as well as they can, given the circumstances, that is behind the economists' presumption of nothing for nothing. It is not ignorance nor stupidity that holds people
back but want of opportunity to acquire and apply knowledge.
When economists present conclusions that imply that actually
more is not preferred to less, or not much more, or that the decision-makers don't really know what they are doing, you should
be aware that they would be doing much better to admit their
own ignorance. That they, the observing economists, are unable
to explain what is going on.

The economists' view of the world does not simply mean that
people do what they do only for the money. Or as economists
would say to consume more goods and services narrowly
defined. They may be doing what they are doing to help others.
But economists would be inclined to see this as helping them-

selves by helping others which should not make such conduct any the less admirable! But economists, with skill developed to recognize trade-offs, or costs that influence behaviour, are inclined to a certain cynicism about apparent and real motives for action which may not always be justified. Nevertheless economists do not have to pretend to explain the behaviour of everybody in all circumstances. They can rely on the law of large numbers, on general tendencies, to undertake analysis that is valid and useful.

Different perspectives on the market for labor

Not all philosophers would agree that economic progress can be made without exploitation. The Marxists hold that employers (the Capitalists to give them their demonic status) get rich by extracting surplus value from their workers. According to the labour theory of value, all the extra output produced by Capitalism belongs to the workers.

The dark satanic mills and mines of the nineteenth century, where the emerging industrial workforce first laboured away, made it hard for the concerned observer to think that these poor and dangerously vulnerable workers, including many working children, were actually doing as well as they could, in the economic circumstances of the time. The real problem, as the classical economists understood it, was the workers' lack of productive – not of bargaining – power. It seemed more obvious to many others, then and since, that the mill owners were exploiting their workers, so seemingly dependent on them for survival, by paying them less than their worth to the employer.

It is as hard today to believe that the squatter camps, so typical of the cities in the poorer parts of the world today, represent economic progress, rather than retrogression. The camps in the cities give access to greater economic opportunity than their poor inhabitants had back in the village. Rural poverty always seems easier to bear than urban hardship, except perhaps for the people who choose the one over the other. The workers of Europe and North America, as we are well aware, have raised their standards of living and the quality of their working environments steadily over time. Regulation of working conditions and employment contracts by social workers, industrial inspectors, as well as the activities of trade union officials, accompanied these improvements in working conditions. These regulations may have followed the better pay and other benefits that competition for increasingly valuable labor brings, or they may have led them. The historical record is not conclusive, as it seldom is whenever cause and effect are difficult to separate.

What seems obvious to economists is that you cannot in some simple painless way legislate for greater productivity. If it were that easy, all that would be required to eliminate poverty everywhere would be the right enabling legislation. Unless workers generally become more productive, working conditions and pay cannot improve for all potential workers. Their pay improves because employers compete away any difference between what any worker is expected to contribute to the output of the firm, or farm, and what it costs to hire them. They do so, not out of kindness, but because other bosses deny them the opportunity to pay as little as they would ideally like. While it clearly makes sense, from an employer's point of view, to pay workers less than they contribute to the firm, other firms which are short of labor, would also like the same opportunity and in their own self-interest bid away what appears as cheap labor. The workers, not to mention the managers, who after all are simply workers with a grander title, are usually well aware of the worth of their hire.

A subset of workers, perhaps the large majority of them, will always survive the impact of any new regulation that makes less productive workers temporarily unemployable. Most, but by no means all the young people of France, who protested in the winter of 1994 against the proposed lowering of the minimum wage for young workers, would have found jobs at the higher minimum wage. The intention was to help the significant number of less qualified young workers who would not be able to do so. By keeping up the minimum wage, the threat of competition from less productive and less well paid workers will have been eliminated.

In the course of time, general improvements in productivity may catch up with the extra costs imposed upon employers. Inflation may also take away from minimum wages and unemployment benefits. The less closely regulated sectors of the economy may absorb the workers who fail to gain the protected jobs, at lower wages or in less favourable conditions, assuming again that these wages offer enough over and above the unemployment benefits. If not, the excluded workers will join the ranks of the unemployed as they have been doing in such large numbers in Europe. Of course some of those classified as unemployed and who are collecting unemployment benefits, will be looking for work. And some will be working illegally.

Temporary labor, employable at lower wage rates, may be substituted for permanent labor. Part-time employment at peak hours may clearly suit both parties. Also, certain functions ordinarily performed within the firm may be sub-contracted to firms less bound by regulation, or union power, if this represents a cost saving to the firm and an opportunity for the staff of the sub-contractor.

The legislation, or regulations influencing employment decisions are likely to have the interests of a politically influential group of workers very much in mind. Typically, well organized and politically influential workers and managers, especially when they work for the government, can make gains at the expense of taxpayers and less well organized workers. Moreover, these favoured and very visible groups of workers may even succeed in representing their gains as being fully representative of all workers, rather than of a privileged minority.

Among the best organized and most politically influential groups of producers are the professions. They are adept at controlling competition for their services and in presenting such controls as being in the public interest. This is not to imply that such controls are not without benefit. The issue is whether such benefits cover their costs and who exactly ends up paying for the benefits. Consumers may be forced to pay more to recover artificially inflated employment costs. However, such gains may also mean less for shareholders should the firm not be able to pass on the unexpectedly higher costs.

The evidence from the countries that industrialized first, is that while the rich were getting richer and there were many more of them, the poor also came to enjoy a significantly improved standard of material well-being. Moreover, expectations of a minimum acceptable standard of living rose as living conditions generally improved.

Yet the poor will always be with us, provided, that is, that some benefit less than others from economic progress. Poverty is surely, in part, a relative concept and so the focus of critical attention has changed from absolute measures of poverty to relative poverty, or measures of income differences between the top 20 per cent of income earners and the bottom 20 or 40 per cent. Most societies appear to exercise a concern for more equal income, as well as more income.

The Marxist prediction that capitalism would collapse because of its internal contradictions has failed. The anticipated contradiction was that because workers were generating all this extra value, but not being paid their worth, they were unable to spend enough. It therefore followed, according to the predictions of Marxist theory, that the economy would suffer periodic crises of under-consumption, when supply exceeded demand. The savings forced from workers would be invested in extra capital, which produced extra consumables, for which there was not enough demand. This lack of demand in turn destroyed the value of the capital created.

There are of course alternative explanations for the business cycle, which recognize the role of misdirected investment and unexpectedly low levels of consumption, yet do not depend upon the labor theory of value. Successful investments have to anticipate demands about which there can be no certainty. Investment firms, in general, may overestimate future demands, or underestimate them. These mistakes, of too much or too little investment – the capital to produce consumer goods – in the plant and machinery, then lead to corrective action by economic decision-makers. Prices rise or fall, as do interest rates, to encourage more, or less, supply and demand generally, of the right kind. Less, or more, overtime is worked and fewer, or more, jobs are on offer. Unemployment rises and falls. These reactions represent themselves as part of the business cycle. The business cycle is one of extended periods of time, when demand and supply are generally increasing at rates above, or below, what may be regarded as a sustainable rate over the long run. A full discussion of the business cycle is undertaken in Chapter 11.

The Leninists tried to save the Marxist prediction that workers would not benefit from unsustainable capitalism, by referring to the presumed role of economic imperialism. The essence of this elaboration of the Marxist position is that, since the workers in the richer countries did improve their lot, they succeeded only by extracting surpluses from the poor around the world. The workers in the industrial world, in unholy alliance with their bosses, improved their incomes by impoverishing the workers in the colonies. In modern parlance, the First World is rich because it has *under-developed* the Third World through a process of *unequal exchange*. The difficulty with the argument is that a country's dependence on trade with industrialized countries is positively, as opposed to negatively, related to their national incomes and average wages. As orthodox economic theory posits, international trade (like domestic trade) enables firms and their workers to become more specialized and therefore more productive and capable of earning more.

Viewing the economic system as exploitative, rather than co-operative, plays on the consciences of the better off and, by so doing, helps those who wish to help the poor, for both charitable and professional reasons. It also helps rationalize the resentment many people feel about the greater affluence of others. It is much more natural to believe that we are much poorer than them because they took it away from us, rather than because they are actually more enterprising, better workers or managers, and so produce more, save more and so earn and spend more. It is a natural response, because for millennia, such an interpretation of large differences in material well-being among neighbours, would often have been true. It is not surprising that explanations of income differences that rely on exploitation or conspiracy theories, should still have so much instinctive appeal.

In previous eras most income was produced on the land. The more land you owned, the wealthier you were. At one time, land was taken away in battle, or given up in exchange for protection against invasion. The original process whereby land was acquired, might therefore be regarded as unfair, or exploitative. Yet today, in the rich countries, agriculture makes a very small contribution to total output and incomes – perhaps 4 or 5 per cent of the value of all output or incomes. It is highly probable also, that the current owners of the land, or their forefathers, traded their own sweat and blood, their savings, for the land acquired originally by some conquering settlers. The original owners, since selling off the family possessions, may well have dissipated their original wealth in an orgy of consumption. Making recompense for some distant original sin of wealth acquisition, be it through expropriation, theft or fraud, is an impossible task and one which few societies even think of attempting. The confiscation, or even expropriation at market value, of land, can make everybody, even those who acquire the land, worse off. Small land owners are quite likely to produce less on their own land than they might have earned working for some large land owner. The land, and the workers on it, are often much more productive and if so, workers will earn more than small land owners.

One of the features of economic development is that workers migrate from agriculture into industry or services, because their labor is more productive and they can earn more there. Another is that, as the economy develops, the agricultural sector becomes more and more heavily subsidized and protected against competition from more efficient farmers at home or abroad. This, of course, raises agricultural output and farm incomes and boosts the price of farming land. The fact that nations and communities still fight each other over land that has so little to contribute to incomes proves that, sadly, man does not live by bread alone.

However, land or income-producing assets generally are acquired fairly through exchange or unfairly through conquest or theft; the wealth owner can choose to conserve the wealth, to add to the original holding by saving and investing some of the income that flows from wealth, or to run down the original wealth by consuming not only the income but the capital as well. There are also opportunities to remove the wealth from one jurisdiction to another, where the locals are expected to be more friendly.

Wealth holders therefore should be encouraged to conserve their wealth and to add to it, rather than to consume it, in the interest of poorer members of the society. Conservation adds to the productive resources of society, which makes poorer workers more productive, while consumption absorbs them. A more productive economy also broadens and deepens the tax base, allowing for more spending on welfare. Any threat of confiscation encourages consumption, and actual confiscation or expropriation penalizes those wealth owners who make a contribution to society while leaving untouched those who consumed their wealth or transferred it away beyond the grasp of any law. That hardly seems fair, quite apart from being economically very damaging.

The same practical considerations apply to the inheritance of wealth. Some would regard it as grossly unfair that anyone is able to lead an idle life in great comfort because of the wealth they have inherited. The practical issue is whether society, or perhaps especially, the bottom 20 per cent of income earners, would have been better off if death duties had confiscated all of the wealth inherited. Clearly, the threat of such confiscation would change savings behaviour dramatically. More would be consumed by the wealth owner bequeathed while still alive, and more transferred to other tax jurisdictions. In addition, the incentive to risk and accumulate wealth might be seriously prejudiced by the threat of taxation during and after life. Usually therefore, the decision to tax inheritance and gifts is decided on practical, as well as ideological grounds. Such decisions will be more or less encouraging for economic growth. The more tolerant the society is of inherited wealth, the stronger the economy is likely to be, all other influences excluded.

The material ethic

An economy has to find appropriate prizes to encourage the competition of new and better with the old, as well as to encourage savings over consumption. Forcing savings, creativity and innovation, or even good repetitive work, does not seem to work as well. The mix of carrot and stick, for different productive processes, will be among the experiments that can be conducted to improve the ratio between inputs and outputs.

It is of course a matter of regret to some, that people need material incentives to deliver more to their compatriots. It might be a better world if we all received according to our needs and produced according to our abilities. Again it is something we may hope for – not to be equal in poverty as we once were, but in great wealth, as we could conceivably be, if only we worked for love of our fellow men and women.

The taste for equality, as well as for greater material welfare, seems to be an important one. The trouble is that nobody, as yet, has come up with the answer to the problem of how to get individuals to produce more, without allowing them to keep much of the extra output for themselves and their own immediate families. Similarly, it seems difficult to persuade members of a community that they have no legitimate claim on the output of others. If the process of creating incomes and wealth is a fair one, relying entirely on capitalist acts between consenting adults,[2] it may be argued that the outcomes – who gets what – should be irrelevant. This, of course, is seldom the case. Contributions to the common pool inevitably become taxes, forced from reluctant taxpayers. How much is taken is almost entirely in practice an issue of politics, rather than of philosophical principle.

Tax rates *vs* tax revenues

Even if the objective of policy is to transfer spending power from the more productive to others, rather than simply to punish the rich and successful, there remain practical limits to tax rates or regulations. In order to transfer as much as is possible from the productive to the less productive, or, if you prefer, from the haves to the have-nots or have less, e.g. from civilian uses to military ones, or from consumption to savings – or more generally from the politically less influential to the more influential – the trade-off between the tax rate and the volume of output (and so the volume of taxes collected) has to be recognized. Tax too highly and you destroy incentives to produce. Tax too little, and you may destroy the incentives fellow members of a community have to protect your incomes and wealth. Such considerations can make willing redistributionists of even the least caring among the more affluent members of a community.

This gives rise to a difficult balancing act which few societies have ever found a comfortable exercise, even when their people have achieved a high degree of material comfort. There is a constant tension between the interest in delivering more goods, which means better rewards for those capable of leading the economy, and the interest in spreading the economic gains around more widely, perhaps more fairly, or usually, just more popularly.

The power to tax, expropriate or regulate, gives all in a society a stake in the output of others. The minority shareholders have to take every care not to extract too high a level of dividend payments, for fear of destroying the incentives of the controlling shareholders and their managers to perform well. Those with control of scarce resources have to make sure that they do not keep too much of the surplus for themselves, for fear of being forced out by hostile shareholders at the next annual general meeting. They are, after all, only the agents entrusted with society's scarce resources, dependent in the final analysis on the approval of the wider community.

Choosing the rules for economic life

Societies decide for themselves how the competition for scarce resources is resolved. They all approach the economic problem in their own way. They develop a structure of institutions, of laws and customs, which establish economic rights. Individuals, or co-operative groups of them, are given the rights to buy or sell goods or services, including those to hire their labor, or to employ, or even to enslave others. Rules will constrain what they may do with their own time and the assets, the capital, they use or own. These rules will determine what part of the output they produce may be kept for themselves and what has to be given up for some collective purpose. Society will not only make and change the rules, but enforce them with degrees of effectiveness.

Within a structure of rights, or what may be called opportunities and obligations, individual economic agents will take economic decisions rationally – that is to say in a logically consistent way. They will, in other words, make the relevant choices, the comparisons between the costs and benefits of alternative courses of action, that will determine what combination of goods and services will be supplied to the citizens, by whom and for whose benefit. The decisions are consequences of the opportunity set, the incentives that the society provides, or fails to provide, for individual economic actors or groups of them. That is why the older name for economics, political economy, was closer to capturing the essential nature of the choices facing society. The big decisions are those taken about the rules that guide economic action. The important choices are political. The rules are decisive for the outcomes. What matters most for economic development are not natural differences between people or places, but the institutions of law and custom that guide humans in this or the other direction – that encourage or discourage innovation of a materially important kind.

Achieving balance in policies

Successful economies deliver more of all the good things to their citizens. In the global village, this does not go unnoticed by voters and politicians in other countries, who feel let down by comparison. The countries that do better at the economic game are capable not only of delivering more to consumers, but to their soldiers as well. Even with the best intentions, they threaten other countries by their very success. They attract the best kind of immigrants, as well as savings from other countries. Since it is their economic policies that are seen to make the difference, these policies encourage emulation. So the more productive are protected, up to a point, by this competition between nations, as well as between regions and towns and villages within regions. The greater the freedom citizens enjoy to move their capital goods and skills across frontiers, the more rapidly are economic policies likely to converge towards the policies adopted in the most successful countries and regions.

This freedom to move people and goods across frontiers does not of course come automatically. Many governments restrict such freedoms to move capital or skills for the *"good of the country"*. Yet they are among the most important freedoms which protect the successful and the enterprising. Ideally, such rights are kept beyond the scope of ordinary legislation and enshrined in a bill of rights and constitutions that governments find more difficult to alter.

Parties, coalitions, special interest groups, even kings and dictators, compete with policies and policy proposals. There are no obvious rules about how countries will make and change the economic rules that are ultimately decisive for economic outcomes. Policies that may be very harmful to economic growth may serve some special interest that is able to prevent change to their own advantage. Not all countries are able to follow the good examples of others and when policies are clearly failing, it may take many disastrous years, even lifetimes, before more productive policies are substituted.

Economic analysis, by exposing the costs and benefits as well as the beneficiaries of different policies, can influence the choices. If people understand the world better, they may make different choices. Economists may be able to influence the collective choices people make through their governments, by identifying the costs and benefits of alternative courses of action. As far as the quality of private or individual choices are concerned, the economist is a mere observer. The economist has no practical advice to offer the worker or the manager. Inside the organization is a big black box in which the engineer, the financier, the accountant, the human resource, organizational behaviour and marketing types weave their magic. It is when the workers and managers emerge from the box and engage with the big world of other businesses and governments, that the economist can hope to offer a better sense of what is going on, so that they can not only survive, but prosper.

1. Perhaps not everybody has laughed at the joke practical business folk like to make about what they would regard as the ideal, one-handed economist – that is one who does not say "on the one hand this may happen, and the on the other hand, something quite different". They are of course appealing for certainties that are simply unavailable. Economists should, at most, claim to be superior forecasters, not clairvoyants. The remark, heard often from practical types by way of criticism of those not part of their world, that something may be "all very well in theory but not in practice", means, in effect, that something is profoundly wrong with the theory. Theory is meant to describe and predict action. and must work in order to be valid. But, to qualify as such, theories must be helpful generalizations about behaviour. A theory is, by definition, something much less than a detailed description of events. It should help observers cut through a mass of detail to get at the essential forces that are driving actions.

2. The author of this memorable phrase is Robert Nozick and is to be found in his important philosophical work, *Anarchy, State and Utopia,* New York, Basic Books, 1974.

CHAPTER FIVE

AN OVERVIEW OF ECONOMIC POLICY

Why Bother?

As workers, managers or shareholders, or when we lend or borrow, or because we pay taxes or receive benefits or subsidies provided by government, the results we achieve will be very much influenced by the overall state of the economy. When the economy grows strongly, all enterprise is encouraged and better rewarded. Jobs are easier to find, the purchasing power of salaries and wages tends to increase more rapidly, funds are more easily borrowed or raised, and the rewards for supplying them improve. Governments, too, become more indulgent in their spending and tax rates may decline. Recessions bring more unemployment and business failures, and often higher tax rates and cut-backs in government spending programs. They are not good times for changing jobs or for starting new ventures. During recessions, wealth owners, including shareholders – and so everyone with a pension or retirement plan, and the many who own their own homes – are likely to suffer from a deterioration in their personal wealth. Clearly, we would do well to anticipate the broad trends in the performance of the economy.[1]

Discretion *vs* Rules

Observing and reacting to the state of the economy is not like watching the weather report in order to decide to dress warmer or cooler, or whether or not to take the car to work. As with the weather, we attempt to anticipate the economic trends and to react sensibly to them. But there is much more to it. The weather, given the available technology, is accepted to be beyond our control. The economy, we are convinced, perhaps too uncritically, is different. Thus governments and politicians are required to accept responsibility for managing and controlling the economy, a task they generally perform with no obvious lack of confidence in the usefulness of their mission.

Economists almost all agree that governments have a crucial role to play in managing the state of the economy. Most are ambitious about what governments could do to help the economy along and believe they should intervene actively to massage total spending. They are of the view that the economic system, if left alone, would be unable to achieve a good balance between the potential supply of all goods and services and demand for them. Consistently with this view of the world, they believe that governments should adapt their own levels of spending and taxes and intervene in financial markets, changing interest rates for example, to eliminate what would otherwise be too little or too much spending. To this end, the authorities are required to make judgments about the current and immediate outlook for the economy and to influence total spending appropriately. That is, to restrain spending when the economy is expected to heat up and to encourage spending when it threatens to cool down.[2]

Other schools of thought would want to see governments do better by abandoning attempts to what is described as "fine tune" the economy. The essence of their argument is that attempts to manage the economy do more harm than good. If the private sector did not have to be concerned with what the government

56

was about to do to the economy, they say, it could more easily and successfully get on with the job of supplying and demanding and the performance of the economy would be the better for it. Thus, members of this school of thought would much prefer to deny discretionary powers over economic policy to treasuries and central banks. Their officers would then not be allowed to manage interest rates and taxes and government spending as they saw fit. Instead, they would be bound by rules compelling them, for example, always to attempt to balance the national budget, or the central bank to achieve some predetermined rate of growth of the money supply. Another possible rule would be for the central bank to maintain fixed rates of exchange of the domestic currency into another currency, or for gold, as under the gold standard. There are arguments between those who are sceptical about the fine tuning capabilities of economic policy – arguments about which binding rule would be the best for the economy: either a money supply rule, or a fixed exchange rate rule.

Some tough policy choices

It is logically impossible for any central bank both to determine the money supply and fix exchange rates, except for short periods until the inconsistency of the multiple objectives reveal themselves. When fixed exchange rates are chosen as an instrument of policy, then interest rates and money supply have to take their cue from the balance of payments. If the balance of payments is in deficit and foreign exchange (forex) is flowing out of the country to pay for the excess of imports over exports, or net capital outflows then, if the trend persists, the country will eventually run out of forex reserves as well as the ability to borrow forex offshore. When this happens, the market takes over the determination of the exchange rate. To prevent this, the country facing a persistent balance of payments deficit, and determined to maintain fixed exchange rates, will have to adopt measures to discourage domestic spending on imports and encourage potential exports, in order to prevent cash from leaving and the forex reserves from declining. Raising interest rates, tax rates and reducing government spending, may all help to restrain spending and improve the balance of payments.

Usually, though, as we shall see, not inevitably, the concern for the balance of payments and the exchange rate is consistent with the broad policy objectives of restraining booms and hastening recovery from recessions. An economic recovery will be associated with more imports and lower exports. The recovery and the extra demands for credit it brings with it, lead to higher interest rates. The actual timing of these interest changes is usually the responsibility of the central bank. If the exchange rate is expected to remain fixed, these higher interest rates will attract more foreign capital and discourage the outflow of local savings and by so doing protect the forex reserves of the country. In a recession the opposite will happen. The trade balance will improve and capital will tend to flow out, so also easing any potential conflict between fixed exchange rates and the state of the economy. The key to stabilizing the system is for the authorities to convince participants in the foreign exchange market that the exchange rate will remain fixed. Higher interest rates mean little if they are expected to be accompanied by currency losses. They are very effective in retaining, or attracting funds, if there is no fear of a devaluation of the currency.

Common currency areas

The States of America are United by free flows of goods money and labor as well as a common currency. A common currency area, which usually means the nation, but sometimes extends beyond national boundaries, is in fact the most highly developed form of a fixed exchange rate system. The adjustment process between the states, or regions of a country, works automatically, though not always painlessly. Money flows freely across the regions in response to changes in demand. Capital, that is accumulated savings, flows from the slower growing regions to the faster growing parts of the country. More precisely, funds or savings are transferred through the financial system, from the households and firms in regions with below average growth, to the firms and households achieving above average growth, which are concentrated in regions that are growing more rapidly. They demand more money and credit to finance their growth. Interest rates have to change very little, if at all, to secure this accommodating movement of funds. They move freely and at low cost through the national financial system, because there is no danger of exchange rate losses.

In a fixed exchange rate system that is not a common currency area, and more so when exchange rates are floating, the danger of exchange rate changes adds to the risks and costs of trade and finance. There is the additional danger that governments may impose exchange controls to protect their foreign exchange reserves. Exchange controls that prevent the payment of interest, or dividends, or the repayment of the capital, add country-default risks on top of the ordinary risks of default by borrowers.

There is little that the slow-growing states or regions of a common currency area can do for themselves to help the process of adjustment. They cannot print money and so they cannot manage local interest rates. The local authorities can, of course, borrow to spend more, but their debts have to be serviced by local taxes. The central government may also transfer funds to slow-growing regions.

Monetary independence

The difference between regions and countries is perhaps obvious. Countries choose their own set of economic policies. Indeed their independence as a nation is defined to an important degree that way. Most independent countries now choose not to fix exchange rates – to tie the value of their own currency to that of another. They prefer to manage interest rates, money supply growth and exchange rates as well as, of course, their budgets. Interest and exchange rates, moreover, are not typically left purely to market forces.

The attempt to maintain fixed exchange rates between the USA and the other major industrial countries was abandoned in the early 1970s. After the Second World War, the industrial world adopted what was, in effect, a dollar standard. The US dollar reigned supreme and other countries attempted to maintain fixed exchange rates with the dollar. Central banks, in turn, could exchange their surplus dollars for gold at a fixed dollar gold price. But, until the Sixties, there was a great shortage of dollars, as the war-damaged countries attempted to reconstruct their economies with the aid of imports from the USA. During the course of the Sixties, the shortage turned to an abundance of dollars, as the USA bought more from, and invested more in, the now fast-growing Japan and Europe. By the late Sixties, the USA, fighting the Vietnam war, and implementing the Great Society welfare system, was forced into making some tough choices.

The choice for America was either to protect the reserves and maintain the convertibility of dollars into gold and other currencies at a fixed rate of exchange, through the application of more stringent monetary policies, or to allow the dollar to float and by so doing, avoid or rather postpone, these adjustments. The USA chose what many economists believed was a brave new world of floating exchange rates. Their belief was that the freedom from the constraints on economic policy, forced by fixed exchange rates, would result in higher average rates of growth. Floating exchange rates, it was thought, gave yet another policy option with which to manage the economy.

Central bankers now adjust interest rates, exchange rates and money supply growth as they see fit, though market forces are by no means necessarily ignored when such decisions are made. For the most part, the movements in exchange rates will conform to the underlying market trends. The participants in the currency and capital markets however, will, in turn, attempt to anticipate the policy choices and so it may become difficult to determine whether the market or the central bank is leading or following movements in interest or exchange rates.

The purpose of a money supply rule is to remove such discretionary powers over interest and exchange rates. The idea is that by choosing to grow the money supply at some predetermined rate, one that ideally would be consistent with very low inflation over the long term, interest rates and exchange rates would be left entirely to the market place. Sometimes, central banks, as part of their discretionary armoury, will announce money supply targets which they hope to achieve over the next 12 months. This is not a rule, as the targeted rate will be chosen with the state of the economy very much in mind.

A case study: Europe in 1992

In the European Common Market, the trend in the Eighties was to closer financial ties and the establishment of fixed exchange rate links between the national currencies and the German mark. Close links to the mark were established, first by neighbouring Belgium, the Netherlands and Luxembourg. Later France and Italy joined a more formalized system of closely tied exchange rates. Britain was the last to link up with this fixed exchange rate system. Maintaining exchange rates within a very narrow range was regarded by Euro-enthusiasts as an intermediate step towards a common currency and a full monetary union.

In 1992 the system faced a crisis. Maintaining the fixed rate of exchange of the pound and the French franc with the D mark, meant having to raise interest rates in London and Paris. The large-scale exchange of pounds and francs for other currencies had begun to put a huge dent into the reserves of foreign exchange, kept largely in dollars, held by the Bank of England and the Bank of France. The problem was that unless these out-flows could be reversed, these central banks would run out of reserves. Raising interest rates, by enough to stop the exchange of pounds and francs for dollars, was the obvious way to protect the reserves. "Enough" meaning whatever increase it would take to convince the speculators that the fixed exchange rate would be maintained.

But Britain and France were both suffering from a severe recession and spending needed all the encouragement it could get from lower interest rates. The speculators were betting that, in such economic circumstances, the politicians would give up the fight for the currency and they were proved very handsomely right.

As indicated, a common currency is a great encouragement to trade and finance, because the risks of exchange-rate changes are eliminated. However, the logic of a common currency is that the European powers, like the American states when they formed their union, would have to give up much of their economic policy independence. They would have, in other words, to transfer

61

their authority for exchange rates and interest rates, and at least partially, their plans for taxes and government spending plans, to some central authority. Consistently therefore, countries hoping, formally, to join the European Monetary Union, were being asked to meet certain goals for their budgets, and the ratio of government debt to the economy, as a condition for membership.

Giving up their economic policy independence however, was something that the major European countries were not ready to do, as the currency speculators knew. The reunification of Germany had earlier put enormous strains on the German budget. The Central Bank of Germany, the Bundesbank, responded to extra government spending and a larger budget deficit by raising interest rates. These higher interest rates made the D mark more attractive, and the pound and franc less so to hold at prevailing exchange rates and so funds moved to Germany. Either interest rates had to rise in Britain or France, or fall in Germany, or the pound and franc had to devalue, or the D mark be revalued. In a truly United Europe, the Germans would have had great difficulty in persuading their fellow Europeans that higher interest rates were called for in the first place. It would also have been European, rather than German taxpayers who would have been called upon to pay for absorbing East Germany into the European benefit system. They might not have been so generous. Quite clearly the European countries did not share enough. Asking them to give up their economic independence, after the Berlin Wall came down and during a recession, was to ask too much.

The short versus the long run

In the end, the politicians decided that, while a single European currency might be best for Europe in the long run, the short-term implications for their economies were too important to ignore. This tension between what is good for the economy and the country on any long-term view, and the political demands of the moment is, as we shall see, the great constant of economic policy.

The view that economic policy should be restrained by rules, is not influential now, and will perhaps be even less so after the debacle of the attempt to establish a common currency for Europe. The central bankers of the major economies have become very confident about their ability to do right by the economy, exercising their judgments if only, as they are convinced, governments would leave them alone to get on with it. They see the major contribution that they can make to the health of the economy, as that of keeping down inflation. They believe that it is by holding down inflation that they can help most to raise the growth potential of their economies. In this objective, they are rather more single minded than they once were. The notion that by accepting more inflation they could help their economies grow faster, has become an anathema.

Governments always feel vulnerable when the economy performs poorly. At which time they are inclined to worry much less about the danger of inflation and much more about getting the economy moving again. This issue of timing and of perceived trade-offs between growth now, for what, it may be argued, will be more inflation later, is the stuff that often divides ministers of finance, or their equivalents, from governors of central banks. It is the reason why the USA gave up the Dollar Standard in 1970 and why the Europeans gave up on their monetary system in 1992.

The strength of the central bank, its degree of independence from government, can be a very useful pointer to the outlook for the rate of inflation. The more independent it is, the lower will be the expected rate of inflation. But the ability of a central bank to withstand pressure from the government depends, not so much on the statutes that establish the central bank, which can always be changed, but on the strength of public feeling about inflation and its consequences. Like all other agents of government, central bankers know that they have to be popular to succeed. Or if not exactly popular, then respected, and not only the morning after. Successfully predicting the state of the economy, in part requires therefore, not only that we know what people and nature are up to, but that we anticipate how the governments and their agencies, particularly central banks, will respond to the state of the economy. We will return to this issue after we have considered further what we and they are up against.

1. The source for all the US statistics referred to is the Citibase, Citibank Economic Database, Machine Readable Data File 1946–92. New York, Citibank N.A., 1978.
2. The acknowledged founder of this approach to economic policy was the celebrated English economist John Maynard Keynes. (1883–1946) The economists who remain faithful to the central vision are known as Keynesians, pronounced Cane-sians. Keynes' most celebrated work was his *General Theory of Employment, Interest and Money,* published in 1936. Keynes himself, paradoxically, was very important in the discussions of and planning for the International Monetary system of fixed exchange rates that would apply after the Second World War. The Bretton Woods system of fixed exchange rates, that would be adjusted only under conditions of fundamental balance of payments disequilibrium, and which applied between 1947 and 1973, was largely his idea. All of Keynes' work and much of his correspondence has been collected in a monumental series of over 30 volumes, *The Collected Writings of John Maynard Keynes,* London, Macmillan, for the Royal Economic Society 1971–1989.

For a recent, two-volume biography of Keynes, see Robert J. A. Skidelsky, *John Maynard Keynes, a Biography*, London, Macmillan, Vol 1 1983; Vol. 2 1993. And for an interpretation that I find particularly persuasive, see Allan H. Meltzer, *Keynes's Monetary Theory: a different interpretation,* New York, Cambridge University Press, 1988.

CHAPTER SIX

SIZING UP THE ECONOMY
Measuring Economic Growth

The size and progress of an economy is most usually measured by its **gross domestic product** (GDP). GDP is the value of the output of all goods and services produced in an economy over a quarter or a year at market prices. Alternatively and equivalently, it is the value of total spending on all the final goods and services supplied to the economy by domestic and foreign suppliers, government agencies, firms and households. What is meant by *final goods* will be indicated below. The market value of output is also equal, by definition, to the value of all the incomes earned by all the resources employed in the production process, again valued at market prices, plus the income taken by government in the form of taxes. That is to say, GDP is equal to the sum of wage, interest, dividend, rental and tax payments made by all firms and organizations, including the government bodies themselves, and this in turn is equal to final expenditures or aggregate demand.

In the inflationary world we live in, GDP has to be adjusted for rising prices, in order to make meaningful comparisons between the size of economies over time and across countries. Real GDP is calculated by dividing GDP, measured, as it is, in money of the day prices, by an index of prices in general. Real GDP is thus an inflation-adjusted measure of the real volume of goods and services produced in an economy over the period. In order to make sense of what is going on in the economy, it is necessary to adjust all nominal, or money of the day, measures for rising prices. What matters to households is their real, inflation-adjusted incomes or purchasing power, that is to say what your salary or wage income buys. Real GDP per head is found by dividing the real GDP by the population.

Between 1950 and 1993, the US GDP more than doubled, and increased at an average compound rate of growth of 2.8%, while GDP per head increased somewhat faster, at 3.4% p.a. on average, over the 40 years. That is to say, the spending power of the average American is now over twice that of the previous generation. This represents very significant economic progress.

The calculation of price indices

The price index used to deflate GDP at market prices – to convert money values into real ones – is called the *GDP deflator*. The GDP is divided by the GDP deflator to provide a measure of Real GDP. It is this real GDP that measures economic progress over time. Unlike the more usually recognized Consumer Price Index (CPI), the GDP deflator indicates how this quarter, or this year's actual mix of output would have been priced in earlier years. The actual mix of production gives the weights to be used in the calculation of the index.

For example, if vehicle production accounted for 5% of the economy (GDP) in 1993, then vehicle prices would have a weight of 5% in the GDP deflator which would be given a value of 100 in 1993, being the year on which the index is based. The weights used in the calculation of the CPI are, by contrast, fixed according to a survey of household expenditure patterns undertaken at ten- or five-year intervals. Thus, if the average household spent 20% of the household budget on food in 1993, when the expenditure survey was undertaken, then food prices will contribute 20% to the CPI thereafter. Or, that is, until the next survey reveals a changed pattern of expenditure. The mix of food items that in turn make up the food price index will be weighted in a similar way with regard to their importance in the family budget. Each country would calculate its own weights, which may differ because of differences in tastes and because *relative prices* – for example the price of cars relative to the price of houses – may differ significantly, causing consumers to choose less of the more expensive items.

The CPI will directly register the impact on the cost of living of rising prices of imported goods, but will not be influenced directly by changes in the prices of exports. The GDP deflator will take account of the prices of goods produced and exported, but will not be influenced by the prices of imported goods. Thus when the ratio of export to import prices changes dramatically, when what is known as the *terms of international trade* improve or deteriorate, the CPI and GDP deflator may give a very different picture of prices and therefore of real incomes. A change in the ratio of export to import prices may be the result of an increase in demand for speculative reasons, or because some natural disaster has dramatically reduced the harvest. Also, some new-found power for a cartel of producers may be the cause of a significant change in the prices of exports or imports.

The terms of trade can influence the exchange rate by causing the volumes of imports and exports to change, but not the other way round. A change in the exchange rate, by itself, has no impact on the terms of trade, because the prices of imports and exports change equally. The best fairly recent examples of such terms of trade effects were for the oil importing and exporting countries, when dramatic changes occurred in the oil price in 1973 and 1979. For the oil importing countries, the rising price of fuel influences the CPI much more directly than the GDP deflator, because oil production is not an important part of GDP. But for countries whose GDP is dependent to a large degree on exports of a particular commodity, in this case oil, the GDP deflator rises or falls much faster than the CPI when the price of the principal export commodity changes dramatically. Another example is provided by South Africa, where gold sales account for between 30 and 40%

of all exports and where the production of gold, measured in money of the day prices, was equivalent to as much as 15% of GDP in the early Eighties, when the price of gold was high. There too, the GDP deflator and the CPI can behave very differently when the price of gold changes dramatically. In such cases, real GDP growth rates, calculated by applying the GDP deflator, which includes the inflated price of the export commodity, to nominal GDP, will tend to understate or overstate the improvement in living standards, as the prices realized for the principal export improve dramatically.

This is because the volume of exports is unlikely to respond immediately to improved, or weaker export prices. But incomes, and especially profits and taxes earned from the export sector, might have changed significantly. But because the volume of exports, or activity, will not have changed much, applying the usual national income conventions would imply that little change in "real" incomes had occurred. Using the lower CPI, rather than the higher GDP deflator, to adjust money of the day incomes to their real equivalent would then give a better indication of the economic realities. For well diversified economies, with a well diversified mix of imports and exports, the use of either a GDP deflator, or a CPI, to establish real magnitudes, will give highly comparable results.

The national income identities

GDP and the other national income estimates are calculated in a more or less internationally standardized way by the national income accountants and statisticians, employed by their respective governments. The basis for the calculations is one of sample surveys of the sales, purchases income and expenditure of all firms or organizations including government bodies and households. GDP may be calculated as the sum of all *value-added*, that is to say the difference between the value of the sales and purchases of every firm (including state owned enterprises) and farm in the country over any quarter or year. The sum of the value-added at each stage of production (value-added = sales less purchases) is, in turn, equal to expenditure on final goods and services. Both are equal, also, to all the incomes earned in the process. That is, incomes earned by the workers and managers, in the form of wages and salaries and other benefits, by suppliers of capital in the form of interest or dividends or profits paid out or the share of profits retained, or by lessors of equipment, or landlords, in the form of their rental or lease income. The income for government, in the form of indirect taxation less subsidies, is also part of total income that is equivalent to the total value of output. The residual item that balances the output–income identity, is profit, or the retained income of business organisations.

GDP, therefore, does not measure total sales, including the sales made by one firm to another, but counts only final sales, that is to say sales to final users of goods and services that are not intended for resale. GDP merely measures the flows of new goods or services produced over a period. The exchange of an asset – a building, or a machine, or a vehicle constructed in some previous accounting period – does not qualify. Only the commissions, profits or salaries earned by the dealers in second hand goods or in financial securities, make it to the national income accounts. These commissions, or the difference between interest income received and paid out for financial institutions, is equivalent to value-added.

A simple table will illustrate the principles at work. Let us start a chain of production with a purely organic farmer. That is to say, a self-sufficient farmer, with a horse drawn plough, who buys in neither fertilizer, nor fuel, and does all her own maintenance and animal husbandry with the aid of some trusty farm workers. She produces $110 worth of wheat, which is sold to the miller. The farmer collects a 10% value-added tax on behalf of the government, ($11) which, it may be assumed, is passed on in the $110 price of wheat. It is of little consequence to any buyer, whether or not a supplier is in fact recovering the taxes in the price charged. All that usually matters to buyers, with alternative sources of supply, is the price, not the profit margin.[1] The miller then processes the wheat into flour, which is sold for $154. The value-added by the miller is $44, and therefore a value-added tax of $4.4 is collected at this stage of the production process. The baker, in turn, adds value, by producing bread, which is sold to the supermarket for $200, representing value-added of $46 plus tax of $4.6. Finally, the retailer adds value equivalent to the gross profit margin of $20 and collects a value-added tax of $2. In addition, the retailer is required to levy a local sales tax of 5% on the bread, which is passed on to the consumer. The consumer then pays $233. Total value-added, including taxes, is thus $233, of which the farmer kept $99 for herself and her workers and paid over $11 to the government. The miller paid out wages, interest and rents to the amount of $40 and $4.4 to the tax authorities and so on. The retailer remitted $2 to the central government and $11 to the local tax collection agency. It may be seen that the sum of value-added, or the contribution to GDP, at tax-included final prices, is equal to the sum of final demands (for bread by households) of $233. The total income earned by individuals and the government may be also seen to be $233 ($200 personal income + $33 government income).

CALCULATING VALUE-ADDED

	1 purch.	2 sales	3 value-added	4 taxes (Income of Govt.)	5 personal income (Wages, salaries, interest, rent profit)
			(2-1)	(10%*3)	(3-4)
Farmer	0	110	110	11	99
Miller	110	154	44	4.4	39.6
Baker	154	200	46	4.6	41.4
Retailer	200	233	33	2+11	20
TOTAL			233	33	200

From GDP to personal income and back again

The national income accountants would subtract payments to

foreign-owned capital, or labour, from GDP and add the income received by domestic residents from foreign sources to get **gross national product** (GNP). This may be regarded as a measure of national income, rather than output. The GNP of a country whose residents have made large off shore investments (net creditor countries) will have a GNP that exceeds their GDP. Similarly, countries dependent on foreign aid, or with a large complement of workers employed in another country, will measure GNP (income) as larger than GDP (output).

When taxes, which add to the market prices of goods, and subsidies to producers, which reduce prices, are subtracted from or added to GDP, the result is **gross national income**. If capital used up in the process of producing GDP – the capital consumption allowance – or depreciation, roughly at a rate of 10–11% of GDP, is then deducted, **net national income** is obtained. Net national income then represents the money value of the goods and services available to the community. Firms may then have to cede a further part of net national income to the government as business taxes, or as contributions to social security funds. A part of national income may be retained by firms as undistributed profits. These undistributed profits, together with the cash retained by the firms and accounted for in their own books as depreciation reserves, constitute the gross savings of business organizations. The cash is retained, rather than paid out in interest, dividends, or taxes or wages or salaries.

Such cash flow may be used to retire debts of the firm, or to make loans to its customers, or may be used to replace or augment the firm's physical plant and capital equipment. Replacing or adding to such physical business capital is regarded as investment spending in the national income accounts. Making loans or buying financial securities, including shares in other businesses, do not constitute investment for national income accounting purposes. They do not represent additions to the stock of physical plant or equipment available to the economy. They are rather the exchange of established assets, or claims on them. For every buyer of a claim, there is an equal and opposite seller. The real stock of capital employed in an economy grows when net investment is positive. It is positive when the value of all investment in newly created and constructed plant and equipment exceeds the rate at which physical capital is used up, that is, consumed, in the process of production.

The **personal incomes** of households include all of national income paid out by the firms to them in the form of wages and salaries, as well as interest, dividends and rentals. In other words, all of national income not retained by the firms as part of their cash flow, or paid to the government as taxes, or contributions to social security funds. The transfer payments made by governments to households, for interest, or payments for welfare, would be additional important contributors to personal income. Interest payments by government, made to corporations, including financial institutions holding government debt, would be included as part of corporate income. Interest payments made by one firm to another, or by households to firms and banks, cancel out in the determination of national income. **Disposable incomes** are then defined as personal incomes, less the deductions made for personal income taxes and personal social security contributions.

The difference between their disposable incomes and the measured consumption expenditures undertaken by households, then constitute personal savings.[2]

In the national income accounts and in the analysis of the broad economic trends, a few broad categories of spending are identified and emphasized. These are the consumption expenditures undertaken by households, which may be broken down further into spending on *durables, non durables and services* (C). The investment spending undertaken by firms and households, mostly on owner-occupied housing. Investment spending by the government, forms another component of final demand (I). The increase, or decline, in inventories held by business organizations, is also identified as a separate category of final demand (S). When inventories increase, an investment is being made and when they run down, disinvestment is taking place. The government consumption spending (G) and net exports (X) – that is, exports less imports of merchandise and commodities and *non factor services*, (for example, insurance premiums, consulting fees, shipping costs, etc.) constitute the other broad components of aggregate demand in the economy. GDP is thus equal to C + I + S + G + X.

Factor services, as opposed to the non factor services that are traded across frontiers, consist of interest, dividend and wage payments made to and received from foreigners. They are payments for the use of resources, of factors of production supplied by foreigners. The balance of factor service payments constitutes the difference between GDP and GNP.

From a national income accounting perspective, government consumption spending excludes so-called transfer payments, that is, government interest and welfare payments that contribute to corporate, personal and after-taxes disposable income and which help finance household consumption.

Government consumption spending (G), therefore, is made up of spending on the public sector workforce and the purchases of goods and services made by government agencies. The difference between tax revenues (T) and this amount then constitutes government saving (T – G). Often G will exceed T implying negative government saving or dissaving. The fiscal deficit, or the borrowing requirement of the State, will be greater than this, as the total government spending to be financed in one way or the other would include all government spending, including interest payments made by the government sector, as well as spending on transfers to households and firms, which national income accountants include as part of personal incomes to be disposed of by households. In the US national accounts, no distinction is made between government consumption and investment spending. All government spending, even on roads and bridges, is treated as if it were resources used up that year. In other countries, following the usual conventions of national income accounting, government investment spending would be added to other investment spending and government saving increased accordingly. The fiscal deficit would be unaffected by such classifications.

Bringing in the Balance of Payments

By definition of the national income identity of output and expenditure, the difference between national income or output (GDP or Y)³, and domestic expenditures, the sum of C+ I+ G (EXP) is equal to the *foreign trade surplus*, or *deficit* (X). That is Y– EXP=X. Thus if domestic expenditure exceeds GDP, it follows that imports will exceed exports by the same amount. Therefore, to improve the trade balance, spending by government, households and firms has to be reduced relative to output levels, and supplies will have to be switched from domestic to foreign markets. Such steps may well be encouraged further by a devaluation. This *expenditure reduction* and *output switching*, in response to a balance of payments problem, may be associated with temporarily more unemployment and excess capacity. This occurs as resources are transferred gradually, in response to the price and profit signals coming from the market place, from firms that specialize in now less profitable sales to the domestic market, to firms that are able to take advantage of what will have become more profitable exports.

Such changes are the ones usually demanded by the International Monetary Fund (IMF) as part of their *structural adjustment* programs. These are designed to resolve the problems of countries that have got themselves into a major balance of payments crisis. The crisis usually means that the country and its banks and firms have run out of lines of credit from foreign banks. In all likelihood, the borrowers will have already reneged on some their obligations to repay loans, or pay interest to foreign lenders, usually banks. The IMF-inspired reforms are rarely popular and what makes them even more unpopular is that they will often require that government subsidies on basic foodstuffs be reduced, or eliminated, in order to discourage domestic consumption and encourage local production. The devaluation of an artificially high exchange rate that will have encouraged imports and discouraged exports, is also likely to be in the package of reforms required by the IMF. Devaluation is also likely to make food more expensive, if foodstuffs have been imported on a significant scale. Countries in crisis are unlikely to regain access to ordinary bank credits without reaching an agreement with the IMF on the structural adjustments required. The incentive to do so, will be a loan from the IMF that will help them over the adjustments and allow them to regain their international credit.

Linking the fiscal and trade deficits

The fiscal deficit, as indicated, is the difference between all government spending, including government spending on transfers and subsidies and tax revenues. This deficit has to be funded either by the government issuing more debt, printing more money, or disposing of government owned assets. Printing more money usually takes the roundabout form of the government selling bonds to its own central bank, in exchange for a deposit with the central bank, upon which the government draws to pay its bills.

The fiscal and trade deficits are linked through the impact the fiscal deficits can have on private spending. The most inflationary method of financing the fiscal deficit is printing money. More money in circulation leads to more spending by the private sector, higher prices, higher imports and lower exports. But even when the funding of government spending is sound – that is, the government borrows in a genuine way and pays enough interest to attract funds from potential private borrowers, or raises taxes – the composition of government spending will remain of crucial importance for the subsequent performance of the economy. When the government itself consumes more, or helps finance the consumption of households through transfer payments, or uses subsidies to hold down the prices of goods and services, domestic expenditure rises and savings fall. Imports will increase and potential exports will be diverted from offshore to the domestic market. In this way, net exports are likely to decline and the trade deficit increase. If the government had, instead, used the funds raised in one way or another to build a road bridge, or harbour, total spending will respond in a similar way, but something valuable will have been left behind to promote output. Both investment spending and savings would have recorded higher values.

A larger fiscal deficit is likely to bring higher interest rates, as the government replaces other borrowers in the financial markets. In this way too, private investment spending declines, or, as it is often described, is *crowded out* by extra government spending. Unless the extra government spending is on the infrastructure of roads and bridges etc., consumption spending generally will tend to be substituted for investment spending, with larger fiscal deficits. The higher interest rates may, however, attract more foreign savings and discourage outflows of domestic savings. The increase in private savings, in response to these higher rewards for saving, is very unlikely to offset the bias in favor of consumption generally that is almost always associated with larger fiscal deficits.

More balance of payments arithmetic

The *current account* of the balance of payments records the foreign exchange used to pay for imports and received for exports, and adds interest and dividend payments paid to foreign equity and debt holders, plus the remittances of expatriate workers and transfer payments that are made in foreign exchange. *Net factor payments abroad*, the difference between GDP and GNP, are not necessarily made in a foreign currency. They include the undistributed profits of foreign owned firms, as well as the income of foreign workers, consumed where they work and not remitted by them, and therefore do not necessarily appear in the balance of payments accounts. The accounts include the flows of foreign exchange to and from the country, undertaken for purposes of investment in financial securities. These flows make up the *capital account* of the balance of payments, which may be positive when inflows exceed outflows, or negative when net foreign investment is being made. By definition, the balance of the flows of all funds across the foreign exchanges, for trade and debt service and independent of trade movements in funds, is equal to the change in foreign exchange reserves, held mostly by the central bank, over the period. When the balance of payments is favourable or unfavourable, these reserves increase or decrease respectively. The central bank or government may also raise loans offshore to bolster the reserves. The true state of the reserves is then revealed by subtracting such loans from the official foreign exchange reserves revealed in the accounts of the central bank or treasury.

In the case of a freely floating, or market determined exchange rate, the balance of payments, taken as a whole, is neither favourable or unfavourable. The exchange rate adjusts continuously, to equalize supply and demand for foreign exchange. A central bank buys or sells foreign exchange, often US dollars, in exchange for its own currency when it intervenes in the market for forex for purposes of managing the exchange rate.

The cause of the trade deficit. Another possibility

It is not only an increase in the fiscal deficit or domestic consumption or investment spending that may lead to a larger trade deficit and smaller capital outflows or net inflows of capital. Should the initiative for capital inflows come from foreigners, who independently wish to invest more in the country, such extra demands for local financial and real assets, especially real estate, will drive up asset prices. The wealth effects of higher prices, which strengthen the balance sheets of households, firms and retirement funds, will encourage domestic spending and borrowing and lead to a decrease in net exports. So, in other words, the capital account surplus may "cause" the trade deficits, rather than the deficits "cause" the capital inflows.

In practice, as in the USA in the Eighties, both forces could be at work simultaneously. The fiscal deficits would have helped keep up interest rates, even while international portfolios were being shifted into US dollar denominated securities, because of their other attractions – perhaps because tax reform made the USA a more attractive location for wealth, or because the Reagan administration's re-arming made the USA a safer haven for capital. The higher than otherwise interest rates, the result in part of additional government borrowing to finance fiscal deficits, made transferring funds to the USA even more attractive than it would otherwise have been.

Real interest rates in the USA from 1981 to 1985 were extraordinarily high and the dollar extraordinarily strong. The very high interest rates of the time strongly suggest that it was the demand for foreign capital from the USA, rather than supply of foreign capital, that was leading the process (see Figure 7). The fiscal deficit and consumption spending were not all that was growing

77

at the time. Between 1983 and 1985 there was an extraordinary boom in private investment spending in the USA, as may be seen below in Figure 20.

Virtue in debt

Developing countries, or rather countries with good development prospects, should be encouraged to run a current account deficit and a capital account surplus. It should perhaps be recognized, however, that the term **developing country** is a euphemism for low income per head country, which may, or may not, have development potential. Foreign savers may be very willing to supply funds to finance the growth in the productive capital of a country with low incomes, and so low levels of savings, but with good development prospects. If the country is to realize its development potential, imports, especially of investment type goods, will exceed exports. The country, or more accurately all the firms located within the country in the process of expansion, will run a deficit on their trade with firms in other countries, as would any firm anywhere, wishing and able to grow faster than their own cash flows would permit. If the investments being financed are well judged, incomes from the expansion of capacity will grow faster than the costs of finance. Repaying loans, or paying interest and dividends will not prove a burden on the borrowing firms, or on the balance of payments of the country.

Savers in mature, and therefore usually slower growing countries, seek better returns offshore, and so would export capital to faster growing regions. Typically, they would run a surplus on the current account of the balance of payments to finance the net offshore investments on the capital account. Usually, the surplus of interest and dividends received from offshore, would be more than sufficient to offset a likely deficit on the trade account of the balance of payments. The USA is clearly not a developing country, so the net imports of capital into the USA during the Eighties and Nineties do not fit into this "normal" pattern.

Japan, despite its economic achievements, continues to maintain very high rates of savings and very large trade surpluses, and exports capital on a similar scale. Also in the Eighties, the

Japanese economy continued to grow rapidly. To join the ranks of the typical developed economy, Japan would have to consume more of its GDP, and save and invest less. It would also have to grow a great deal more slowly than it did for much of the Eighties. As will be indicated below, the level of transfer payments made by the Japanese government, is exceptionally low by developed country standards. This reluctance to make welfare payments, is clearly the major reason for the high rate of saving and investment in Japan.

Some problems with the measurement and interpretation of national income accounts. Identifying causes and effects from the statistics

Any identity or equation of the national income or balance of payments kind, is what economists describe as an *equilibrium condition*. It is a situation where supply and demand for goods and services (the national income identity), or for foreign exchange (the balance of payments identity), are equal. But there can be no presumption from any observation of the identity, that supply causes demand, or demand causes supply. Both, together, determine the level of prices and output. They act together like the two blades of a pair of scissors.[4]

The task of economic analysis is to get behind demand and supply. This enables proper to separation of the initiating cause from the subsequent effects on prices and output that bring supply and demand for an individual good, or for all goods and services, or for foreign exchange, or labor, into balance. The discussion of the causes of the US twin deficits, fiscal and trade deficits, above, was one such attempt. The direction of price or interest changes, as well as output levels, is more revealing than the fact that supply and demand are always measured as equal. That on any stock exchange day, or minute, the number and value of shares sold is always equal to the number bought, is of little importance. What matters to investors is the price change and to the brokers the turnovers, not the equality of supply and demand. Stockbrokers prefer rising prices, or bull markets, because they bring higher turnovers.

Presenting one or other side of the national income, balance of payments, or money supply equations, as constituting an explanation, or a cause, rather than as something true by definition of the accounting system, can be misleading. The best example is perhaps that when the state of the economy is reported and analyzed, the national income identity is typically set up as demand causing supply. This emphasis on demand causing supply is not of course coincidental. National income accounting analysis dates from the 1930s when lack of demand, rather than a shortage of supply, seemed to be the major economic problem. Until the Sixties, much of the discussion of economic policy in the developed world continued to take pretty much for granted that the problem to be sorted out was that of too little spending. This bias has largely been retained and is reflected in the presentation and discussion of national income updates. The idea that excess demand necessarily causes the trade deficit is part of this emphasis. Modern supply side economics, which emphasizes the forces (especially tax rates) that influence decisions to supply, is a reaction to this.

Reconciling the accounts

Total output in the economy will always equal total expenditure, by definition. The balancing, or *residual* item that makes them equal, by definition, in the national income accounts, is the way investment spending is defined, to include spending on inventories. If total spending falls unexpectedly, because households or firms wish to save more, and so the structure of production is not perfectly adapted to the changing mix of potential demand, *inventories*, that is supplies of materials to be used in production or finished goods awaiting delivery, will rise automatically. The lower level of spending will have led automatically to more investment in inventories. And so demand, including demand for additional inventories, will be calculated as equal to supply. But orders will dry up for the goods of which the retailers, and others, are carrying an excessive inventory. Profits and output in the affected firms and industries will decline as resources are reallocated. Subsequently, measured incomes and so savings may well fall, as the adjustment of the mix of production in response to less spending and more saving is made. More real savings may mean lower interest rates, which, in turn, would encourage more investment in real plant and equipment. The extra savings may flow to other economies, if returns there appear superior. This means that separating an intended from an unintended increase in inventories is vital, if the national income statistics are to be used to predict the direction of the economy. When consumption and investment spending picks up speed, inventories are likely to fall, so temporarily reducing the growth in measured GDP. When final demands slow down unexpectedly, inventories will increase, so holding up measured GDP until production adapts to the lower demand.

On the income side of the national income identity, which equates total output, incomes and final expenditures, the savings and profits of the household sector are the balancing item. If demand and output grow slower than expected, then profits automatically decline to balance the books. In national income accounting practice, as has been indicated, personal savings are estimated as a residual that matches estimated expenditure with estimated income. The difference between income and expenditure is defined as personal savings. Furthermore, in practice, it is extremely difficult, if not impossible, to separate the business from the other economic activities of households. For this reason, unincorporated businesses are regarded as part of the household sector. Thus, the retained profits of unincorporated businesses end up as part of personal savings. Any statistic derived as a residual, or balancing item, is unlikely to be very reliable. Any errors in estimating the other items will be reflected in the residual which make measures of personal saving not especially reliable.

The somewhat independently calculated estimates of final output and estimates of final expenditure, have to be reconciled. Since they are measured in different ways, the numbers will not balance exactly. Ideally, such balancing items should not have any obvious bias one way or the other. But the incentive to evade taxes, as well as any lack of record keeping and reporting procedures, may well introduce such biases. Expenditure estimates may prove consistently larger than income estimates, if there is a tendency to under-report income rather than spending. If so, national income measures should best be adjusted upwards to fall in line with the estimates of final expenditure rather than the other way round.

It is likely that incorporated businesses, rather than households and unincorporated businesses, will keep the better records. Businesses, after all, incorporate themselves because of the advantages of limited liability when they raise capital. But to raise capital from the banks, or the public, requires a higher standard of reporting. And so the owners have to be willing to expose more of the enterprise to inspection by outsiders and to provide more reliable statistics. The IRS, as well as the national income accountants, come with the territory. The income and output generated by the informal sector of the economy is, by definition, not recorded, and may be very important in the total scheme of things. Estimates of the size of unrecorded activity in different countries vary, from as little as 5, to as much as 40% of GDP.[5] In Italy, which has a large unrecorded economy, there was national rejoicing when large official estimates of the informal sector were added to GDP. Suddenly the Italian economy had moved ahead of Britain in the economic league.

What do the numbers really mean?

More fundamentally perhaps, it should be appreciated that GDP measures the quantity of output as the means to the end, not so much of consumption, but of the benefits of consuming. It is quantity, rather than quality, that is being observed. The resources devoted to keeping people warm in winter and cool in summer and getting them to and from their work, may represent a significant part of GDP, depending on climate and locale. People clearly choose where they live and work and their mix of spending. But some of the choices they make must be regarded as representing costs rather than benefits. They spend more time on the heavily subsidized train to work, as a trade-off for higher salaries in the big city. Such considerations make it much harder to make comparisons about the standard of living across time and between countries or regions using GDP or GDP per capita. A better comparison might be made using consumption per head, including the consumption of time spent at leisure rather than having to commute to work. There are alternative measures of the standard of living – for example of life expectancy or calorie intake or ownership statistics – that may provide very good insights about improving living standards. Yet all these measures will tend to be highly correlated with the growth in GDP per head.

Problems with the conversion to constant prices

Some measurement problems are compounded when the conversion of the estimates of expenditure, or output, from their money of the day values, to their real equivalents is made. It is easy to convert consumption, investment and government spending from money of the day to their constant price equivalents by applying the appropriate consumption, investment and government expenditure deflators. It is not possible to make the same conversions with changes in inventories, or any of the residual items. The real changes in inventories and in the other balancing items, are treated as balancing items linking the estimates of real expenditure and real output. Thus, it becomes impossible to interpret differences between nominal and real changes in inventories, savings and the other residuals. Changes in the measured, real, residual items can make a significant impact on quarterly growth rates. Thus it has been my experience in South Africa, that successfully forecasting the state of the economy from one quarter or year to the next, is not only, or necessarily, a matter of forecasting what will happen to final demands (C + I + G + X), but of forecasting the residual, which in theory should have an expected value of zero. For this reason, the emphasis given in my own forecasting exercises, has been on attempting to forecast the annual growth in nominal final demands. Then, as a separate exercise, to forecast the deflators, or inflation rates to be used to convert nominal values into their real equivalents.

Exchange control and the balance of payments accounts

Balance of payments statistics are likely to be highly inaccurate for countries that impose exchange control. Any recorded distinction between payments for trade, debt service, or capital movements is likely to be moot. With the cooperation of trading partners abroad, or by controlling enterprises there, savings can be shipped offshore by under-reporting exports receipts, or over - invoicing imports. The excess is saved in a foreign bank account. Similarly, dividend, or interest payments, if more freely allowed than repayments of principal, may well largely represent capital transfers. The domestic personal savings measure can be much distorted by such hidden transactions.

The upshot of all this is that quarter-to-quarter estimates of GDP are subject to significant measurement errors. Significant revisions of the first estimates are often made. Furthermore, the accuracy and reliability of the estimates rely greatly on the formal accounts kept by established businesses. Where the share of formal business in the economy is small, or changing rapidly, or where there are strong incentives not to report the economic facts, the national income statistics have to be treated with particular caution. All in all, the numbers mean less than the trends. GDP should best be regarded as an index of economic activity, rather than an accurate measure of the economy – and then only for countries with well developed markets and a stable economic structure. Furthermore, the longer term trends are likely to tell more than levels, or changes in levels, from quarter to quarter. Yet for all the reservations one can have about the meaning of GDP, it is the best single measure we have, and there is absolutely no sign of any other notion of overall economic activity replacing it.

1. If the buyer is dependent on the seller as a sole, or important source of raw materials or services, then the profit margins and so the survival of the supplier will be important to the buyer.
2. In practice, personal or household saving, which includes the savings of unincorporated business enterprises, is measured as a residual, as being the difference between disposable income and

consumption, rather than surveyed independently. Thus any tendency to under-record incomes will reveal itself as a lower level of personal savings. That is, the impact of the under-recorded incomes is likely to be revealed as higher levels of recorded consumption spending. Since income is likely to be taxed at higher rates.

3. GDP is usually labelled as Y in the economics literature.

4. This expression was introduced by Alfred Marshall, Professor of Economics at the University of Cambridge in the late nineteenth and early twentieth century. His *Principles of Economics* (1890) dominated the field for many years.

5. One indirect method used to measure the informal sector, is to draw inferences from the demands for money. The demands for, and supply of cash are known to be closely related to incomes. Money demands are measured as dependent on incomes, interest rates and the evolution of the payments mechanism. Supplies of money in excess of such estimated demands are then used as a proxy for unrecorded incomes.

CHAPTER SEVEN

IDENTIFYING ECONOMIC POTENTIAL OR ITS ABSENCE

Revealing some important trends

In this chapter we identify some of the important signs to look for in order to be able to decide whether a country is getting it more or less right. The issue is one of degree – of more, or less, of the right stuff. There are issues about getting going, which are the problems facing the poorer parts of the world. There are also the economic problems faced by the advanced industrial countries. They have truly magnificent economic achievements to protect and also to build upon. It is mostly the issues confronting the well-developed economies that are dealt with here.

Incentives not resources

The ability of an economy to deliver more goods and services over time will depend very largely on the incentives provided by the society for different categories of people – workers, managers, entrepreneurs, government officials, savers and all who participate in the economy to do right by the economy. Doing right means that a larger percentage of the potential work force will wish to be employed. The fuller participation of women in the labor force, as well as the transfer of workers from rural self-subsistence to the modern sectors of the economy, have both played very important roles in promoting economic growth. The incentive to save, rather than consume incomes, is vitally impor-

86

tant for economic growth. Doing right, by providing the necessary incentives for the firms and their owners to absorb more risk and invest in productive assets, will be crucial if workers are to be made capable of producing more and earning more.

The gap between the before and after tax rewards for working, saving and investing, will be of the greatest importance in encouraging work effort, discouraging consumption and encouraging investment and risk taking. The quality of services provided by the government, in exchange for the taxes collected, will be important too in influencing the contributions that are made to the economy. The quality of service provided by the people who work for government, in relation to the cost of employing them, is important for the taxpayer and the consumer of services. The sense of security of life and property experienced by economic actors is also very much part of the incentive system.

Particularly important will be the establishment of a good system for linking economic achievement and rewards. A market-driven meritocracy, rather than a system of access to work and rewards based upon some traditional, or political status, will be absolutely necessary in providing the right signals. The development of a financial market, to link savers and investors and encourage economic specialization, but which is also able to monitor the performance of managers, is crucially important, if the economy is to advance. The economy benefits from competition for savings, workers, managers and for resources generally. Not only should markets generally be contestable by newcomers, but the right to control established firms, especially large firms, should also be made subject to the market test for survival.

Governments can get in the way of market-determined outcomes, for all sorts of reasons that may make excellent political sense, but are not good for the economy. In the final analysis, it is policies, rather than the national character of the people, or an endowment of natural resources, that matter for economic development. There are a large number of case studies of countries, where the economic outlook for the people who live there has been transformed completely, within a generation, and a still larger number have yet to do so. There are no economic miracles, only the right or the wrong kinds of economic policies.

Identifying some important trends:
savings and investment, imports and exports

The share of national income invested will largely determine the stock of capital and the productivity of the workforce. Foreign savings and investment might also play an important role in augmenting the capital available to the workforce. The great bulk of the savings used to finance investment in a developed economy, is typically found from domestic sources. Foreign capital played a crucial role in the early development of the USA, Australia, Argentina and South Africa, as it is now doing in China and other parts of Asia.

The share of exports and imports in the economy will indicate the gains that have been made from international trade and the degree to which firms and households have become more specialized and therefore more productive. A large import and export sector indicates that the barriers to international trade have been unimportant. The greater the importance of international trade, the more effective will be the competition for local producers and consumers. When the market is effectively the world market, there is little scope for any one firm to dominate it. Small, open economies have little scope for, or need of, anti-trust legislation. If their own firms are to be competitive in the world market, they will almost inevitably be large firms, in order to enable them to realize the required economies of scale. If so, they will be the dominant domestic producer. But effective competition for such local "monopolies" will come from abroad. If the market is the world market, then there are no monopolies and the case for anti-trust falls away. The smaller the geographic area that is defined as the market, the fewer competing firms that will be found there. A small village is unlikely to have more than one shop.

The last thing economic policy should be doing, if it wants to encourage the ability of its producers to compete internationally, is to attempt to restrain the growth of its own winning companies because their success allows them to dominate the local market. Small economies are likely to be more open than large ones. If the domestic market is very large, as is that of the USA and

Japan, many of the available economies of scale may be achieved by domestic, rather than foreign sales. This size-of-country factor should be taken into account when the degree of openness to trade is used as a criteria for measuring the economic efficiency of different economies.

Thus the trend in the investment and foreign trade to GDP ratios may give important clues about the longer run potential of an economy. The ratio of gross domestic savings and investment in the USA has declined in recent years from between 15 and 20% of GDP in the Sixties and Seventies to well below 15%. These are very low ratios by international standards.[1] Such savings trends for the USA must be regarded as unpromising for faster growth in US incomes per head. Yet the US economy has been outstandingly good at increasing employment and absorbing labor, by comparison with most other major industrial economies, which have failed to increase numbers employed and also, typically, to register much higher unemployment rates.[2]

The US record in improving the output per employee has been less impressive. Improvements in the productivity of the work-force may come from better management, as well as more capital. It remains to be seen whether the much heralded benefits of downsizing and information technology and the strength of venture capital in the USA, can overcome the disadvantage of a low and declining rate of saving and investment.

Exports and imports have come to play a more important role in the US economy with exports rising from the equivalent of about 5% of GDP in the Fifties and Sixties to about 10% of GDP today. Imports have grown slightly faster than exports. Thus by definition the trade deficit and net foreign capital inflows have increased (see Figure 1). The USA has become a much more open and therefore competitive economy in the past 20 years.

The adjustment to the forces of international competition has been particularly difficult for the labor force in the older manu-facturing industries – vehicles and steel – in which US firms were once far ahead of the competition and their workers by far the best paid industrial workers anywhere. This is no longer the case.

On the definition of Savings and Consumption

An improvement in the skills of the labor force is vital for economic growth. Spending on education and training may be regarded as an investment in people if it enhances their earning potential. Such spending is, however, regarded as consumption spending in the national income accounts. Spending on education should surely be defined as investment in human or intellectual capital, the benefits of which are not consumed overnight. If spending on education were regarded as investment, then measured consumption spending would be lower and savings higher. But spending on investment, including spending on education and training, is only one dimension. While it does indicate the

Fig. 1

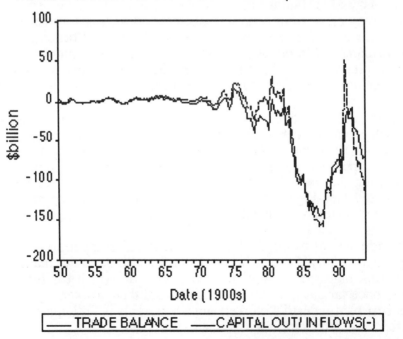

TRADE BALANCE AND CAPITAL OUTFLOWS (-CAPITAL INFLOWS)

sacrifices of consumption that are being made, it does not, in itself, tell us anything about the quality of the investment decisions. In the case of private investment spending, firms go broke if the investments are ill-judged. The same discipline does not always apply to government investment, including spending on education, or any other component of government spending which may prove a wasteful use of resources.

Economic growth depends on the quality, as well as the quantity of spending on investment goods. It is much harder to measure quality when there is no obvious measure of performance to be reported. Such concerns apply in an extreme way, to spending on education and training, where the association between greater inputs and outputs seems to have been particularly perverse in many developed economies. Introducing competition for government-subsidized students, between schools, universities and training establishments, as an alternative to indiscriminate funding, is an obvious solution to the problem of getting value for money in educational spending. But such reforms, in the US and UK, are being frustrated by the educators, who have the usual powerful interest in the status quo. Opposition has also come from those, for example in the American suburbs, who have been able to maintain quality within their own independent school districts and who see reforms as an unnecessary threat to their own achievements.

Countries will increasingly compete through the quality of their labor force. The ability to reform education in the interest of the consumers, rather than the producers of educational services, will divide economies. A measure of the competitiveness of the educational system, that is, of the degree to which the educators are competing with each other for custom, will be a useful indicator of economic growth.

A strong case can be made for classifying household purchases of durable consumer goods – furniture and appliances, or cars – as investment, rather than consumption. If the household leases rather than owns a new appliance or car, the spending by the leasing company on the new equipment used by the household, would be classified as investment. Such distinctions are clearly arbitrary and may distort comparisons of savings and investment ratios across countries. Actual consumption spending, that is, the value of the consumption services received, from a washing machine, or hi-fi set, is equivalent to the lease payments made. The lease, or rental payment, explicit or implicit, is the price of consumption. These payments must cover depreciation and maintenance and provide a return on the capital employed. When households own, rather than rent, they are consuming roughly at the rate equivalent to a leasing charge. Ideally, such imputations should be made to measure the value of consumption of consumer durables. It would be more revealing of the character of the economy if purchases of new items of household capital were regarded as investment and the depreciation of the stock of household capital were added to the allowance made for capital consumption generally.

Government Spending, Taxes and Transfers

As may be seen in Figure 2, the ratios of government expenditure and tax revenues to GDP in the USA have risen. The growth in expenditure has exceeded revenue growth, so causing the fiscal deficit to increase as a proportion of GDP.

Welfare payments have become much more important in the US government budgets and the economy, rising from only 4% of GDP in the Fifties to nearly 16% of GDP today. Interest payments by government have, by contrast, remained a relatively stable share of the economy.[3]

One of the regular features of economic development is that, as an economy grows, government expenditure, tax revenues and transfer payments tend to increase faster than GDP. National incomes per capita, measured in US dollars, can help to predict the ratio of government spending to GDP.[4] It would seem clear, that it is higher levels of incomes and therefore the ability of governments to raise more tax revenues, that causes the share of government in the economy to increase, rather than the other way around – more government spending causing higher growth. Much more will be said below on the relationship between government spending and economic growth.

Fig. 2

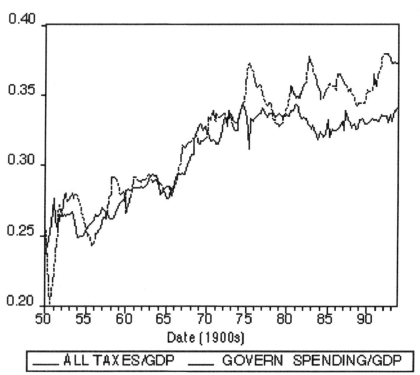

More interesting perhaps than the general tendency for the government's share of the economy to rise as the economy develops,
are the deviations from the cross-country norm. The countries
that maintain a role for government that is significantly less than
would have been predicted by income per head, may be presumed to have superior growth prospects. The example of Japan,
with an exceptionally low level of transfers compared to the
norm, is a striking one. It is noticeable that some of the slowest
growing economies are among the countries with actual transfer
ratios above predicted levels.

The Swedish economy, one of the most highly developed in the world, and with an extraordinarily high level of government expenditure, especially on transfer payments to its citizenry, was once regarded (by many economists) as an ideal model for others to emulate. The Swedish model is now conspicuous for the difficulty Sweden is experiencing in paying for the benefits that have come to be expected by the people. Such expectations undermine incentives to work and save and by so doing reduce the size of the economy and the amount of tax that can be collected. High taxes tend to raise the costs of labor and capital, making it much harder for Swedish companies to compete effectively in both their home and foreign markets, with producers who are burdened with less tax. This, too, reduces the size of the economy and the ability to collect taxes.

More and more of the expenditure of government has then to be financed by borrowing. This extra borrowing then means that more and more of the taxes collected, and loans raised, have to go to pay interest, rather than to provide benefits. And the loans increasingly come from abroad, making it necessary for Swedish business to earn foreign exchange, not so much to pay for imports, but to pay interest on government loans. Clearly the situation has become untenable and adjustments to the welfare system have to be made, with the result that some Swedes are able to pay for the benefits others receive. Naturally, such adjustments are proving very difficult to make.

European countries typically have governments which play an exceptionally large role in economic life by comparison with the USA, or Japan. The government's share of the US economy is below the international norm, but as we shall consider below, this may well change should health care reform proceed. If Japan is to become a "normal" rich country, it would have to indulge its own people with welfare benefits on the scale of the trading rivals with whom it has competed so successfully.

The effective tax rate of a country may be regarded as the ratio of all taxes to GDP. Governments of richer countries, spend and tax and transfer a larger share of their economies than the governments of less wealthy countries, presumably because they have the capacity to do so. Higher tax rates, in themselves, must discourage private savings, investment and risk taking. Clearly, if governments provide for unemployment, illness, accidents and old age, as well as providing basic subsistence and housing, as they increasingly do in developed countries, the incentive to save and work is diminished, with further negative influences on economic growth.

While the direction of the impact of higher taxes on savings, enterprise and work effort is clear enough, giving precision to estimates of such effects is very difficult. Just how sensitive the supply of savings, labor and risk taking is to lower after-tax rewards, is an empirical issue that cannot be easily resolved by economic analysis. As with most attempts to provide precise answers to such important questions, there are always a number of forces at work that are difficult to isolate from each other. The most that even the best empirical work in economics can do, in resolving the big issues of this kind, or perhaps any issue in economics, is to be suggestive, or supportive, of the underlying thesis. Economics is an art, because the issues cannot be resolved in controlled experiments conducted in a laboratory. The best experiments are perhaps those conducted by other countries and the appropriate method, one of examining such case studies.

Taking budgetary strain

Given the difficulties in raising extra tax revenues, and the political attractions of welfare benefits, or entitlements, it is government spending on infrastructure and education that may be sacrificed for the sake of a better balance between government spending and taxation. If so, this would provide another example of the long-term interest of the community in more capital, and so more output, over time, being sacrificed for more consumption now. The interests of the old in consumption now, may prove more influential than that of the young in more investment now, so that they may produce more and consume more later. Future generations lose out when less is invested and more is consumed. The actual method the government uses to finance its spending – taxes vs debt vs money creation – is only important for the secondary effects it has on the consumption, savings and investment decisions that are being taken now. Government debt used to finance government spending is neither a burden nor of benefit to future generations. But they will suffer from a lack of investment.

Fundamentally, the burden (the negative effect on their wealth), for taxpayers of a tax now, or a series of taxes later that will have to be collected to pay the interest on the extra debt, will be exactly the same. If the tax bill for an extra $100m of government spending were presented now, or presented as a series of tax bills to meet the interest payments on an extra $100m debt, the present value would be precisely the same – $100m. On the national balance sheet, domestically owned government debt is both an asset and a liability. The tax payments of some, are the interest receipts of others, and the assets and liabilities cancel out. Government debt sells for the present value of the interest payments being offered, in exchange for cash now.

The issue is therefore not how the government finances its spending, but how resources are allocated between consumption and investment spending. The problem with paying interest on debt, is that taxes have to be raised to do so. Such taxes are as unpopular as any other taxes. Thus, investment spending, including spending on education, that could leave a legacy, may be sacrificed to maintain spending on what are more popular entitlement programs that encourage more consumption spending, and so less saving and investment. In the same way, resorting to debt, rather than tax finance may initially make it easier to increase government spending, but as the debt issues accumulate, the ever-rising interest payments become a trap from which the government budget has great difficulty in extricating itself.

The limits to taxation

One possible way out is to pass a rule requiring that the government budget be balanced. Applying this rule prevents the exercise of the easier financing option, but it does not necessarily mean that government spending will be directed more towards investment spending and away from consumption. It may well mean the opposite. It might in fact be better for the encouragement of public sector investment spending, and so economic growth, to restore the traditional distinction between the capital and current accounts of the government budget. Capital items, for example bridges and roads, which generate future income or benefits, are appropriately financed by loans. Consumption should be financed by taxes. It was probably the view that what is most important about government expenditure, is the contribution it makes to demand, irrespective of what the government actually buys, that encouraged the consolidation of the government accounts into one cash budget.

Foreign debts are different. Foreign liabilities do not cancel out on the consolidated national balance sheet. The debt is owed to an outsider and the community as a whole has to save more to pay back foreign debt. If the foreign borrowing was used to finance an investment, then the national balance sheet will show this as an asset to balance the liability. If, however, foreign loans were used to finance consumption spending, there will be nothing to show on the asset register and no extra income will be available to help pay back the loan. The result may well be, later, greater misery, as the creditors, led by the International Monetary Fund, take over the management of the bankrupt economy.

Privatization

Instead of issuing more debt, governments may sell equity. That is, they may sell off part, or all of their stakes in government-owned business enterprises. They may elect to privatize what was previously nationalized, or to sell off to the public businesses originally established by the government. In a number of countries outside the centrally planned economies government ownership and control can be all-pervasive. Government-owned organizations supply power and telephone services, railroads and airlines, steel and motor vehicles. Banks and insurance companies may be government-owned too. Such businesses typically operate on the same general principles as do privately owned firms, by charging for their services and by attempting, not always successfully, to cover their costs. They are also often protected by their governments from direct competition and constitute a government-owned and -sanctioned monopoly.

The more these organizations are expected to cover their costs, the more they will be worth in any sale. Thus the temptation, for a government seeking as much revenue as possible, is to make the sale with the monopoly powers entrenched. This clearly sets up a conflict between the consumer and the taxpayer, though in many cases, especially that of the more important utilities, they may be the same people.

In practice, and despite the protection against competition that may have been provided, government-owned businesses may well have made operating losses, rather than profits. Rather than paying dividends to the state, they may have received large subsidies from it. The reason for this state of affairs was seldom because consumers were receiving an especially good deal, but because the managers and workers had managed to capture control of the enterprise for their own purposes. Compared to the rest, wages and salaries, as well as working conditions and job security, often made employment within state-owned organizations highly desirable. Politicians naturally attempted to use the state's control as a further instrument of patronage.

The state-owned enterprises were originally established for political reasons and it is the political interests that keep them going. Any move towards privatization has to override such established interests. A financial crisis for the state, combined with a strong sense on the part of the voters of having been abused by state-owned businesses, may be helpful to the process. The losers are bound to be the established workforce and the winners the consumers, if the newly privatized organizations are forced to compete for the latter's custom. The role that the new shareholders will be allowed to play, in disciplining the managers of their enterprise, is likely to be crucial in determining the success of privatization. A few important shareholders would be much more likely to encourage good management. But any such concentration of control may be disallowed in the interest of spreading share ownership. Such arrangements will leave power largely with the managers.

The revenue implications of privatization are perhaps less important for the economy in the long run than whether or not the newly privatized firms and the resources they employ are well managed. Taxpayers, as consumers (whether direct or indirect), will be best served if the assets that are being disposed of on their behalf, are made subject to the full forces of competition. This would mean no restrictions on other firms competing, or on powerful shareholders, or groups of them, taking control.

The paradox of wealth

There is a paradox with government budgets that has to be resolved. It is only the rich countries that can afford to pay for welfare transfers on a significant scale. It appears therefore, that the construction of a transfer system does not prevent, even if it may slow down the rate of, economic growth. But even so, it still needs to be borne in mind that the standard of living achieved by citizens of the developed world is very impressive. Growth has slowed down, but off a very high base.

The economic problem of the rich countries of the world is ironically largely an embarrassment of riches. The real problem is the growing dependence of an increasing number of their citizens on a welfare system, which largely provides for material needs and undermines the incentives to work, save and be enterprising. Welfare payments have become less a support-system for people in an emergency, and more a permanent system of benefits, to which large numbers of the citizens are entitled and of which an increasing proportion avail themselves. Only the high levels of incomes achieved in the developed world and, so, the potentially large tax base, can provide assistance on such a vast scale. But even so, the politicians in countries that have taken the welfare state furthest, are now being forced to recognize the limits to their ability to extract more in order to pay for popular benefits.

In some ways, welfare payments may contribute to growth prospects. For example, by providing a less costly alternative to still more damaging wealth transfers (nationalization and expropriation of assets), they may promote tolerance for enterprises which generate incomes both small and large, as well as savings and wealth. Also, by spending more on health and shelter, the workforce will have become healthier, and therefore more productive. It should be appreciated in addition that taxing and spending by governments is not just about taking from the rich to give to the poor. The great bulk of taking and giving is likely to be from middle income people, at a certain stage of their careers, who then receive much of it back in retirement, or when sick, or through their children's education. Government spending on education, especially tends to favour the more naturally talented, or better nurtured, children of middle and higher income parents. The poor leave school early.

But clearly, a balancing act is required of societies. Welfare transfers must not give too much, and especially not too much too soon. They must follow, rather than disrupt, the achievement of a stronger economy with higher income per head. As is becoming apparent also, they can then easily be overdone and reach a point at which the economy stagnates or, worse, shrinks.

When enough becomes enough

The stresses on the welfare system become particularly severe when growth, for whatever reason, perhaps unrelated to domestic economic policy, slows down and unemployment increases. During recessions, the payment of generous unemployment benefits can strain the government's budget severely. It is estimated that the cost of unemployment benefits in the European Union in 1994 will be $250b – an amount larger than the GDP of Belgium. At a conference in 1994 organized by President Clinton, for the so-called Group of 7 countries, to discuss unemployment, it was estimated that 30m people from the G7 countries were unemployed.[5] Taxes may have to be increased in order to avoid the interest on the government debt trap referred to above. But further tax increases, designed to help the budget, make the economy even more vulnerable to foreign competition from countries with a less generous welfare system, and so, lower taxes.

Higher income taxes reduce the supply of capital and labor and make capital, and especially skilled labor, more expensive. This is seen, in particular, when both capital and labor migrate, as they will do, in search of a better combination of after-tax income and the benefits of government spending. If firms are to remain profitable, they have to recover the higher, tax-induced costs of capital and labor from their customers, in both local and foreign markets. If they are unable to make these recoveries, they eventually go out of business and the ranks of the unemployed grow more numerous still. The problems of the economy become compounded.

On or off the budget

In order to prosper, firms also need to be able to recover from consumers or workers the cost of satisfying regulations and other mandates imposed on them by government. These costs are equivalent to a tax increase, but they are off the government budget. If firms are unable to recover the costs from consumers, in the form of higher prices, they either claw back from the shareholders of the firms, or from the workers – by paying them lower money wages.

If the economy is to remain competitive, raising indirect taxes, by, for example, increasing the value-added tax rate, as an alternative to higher income taxes or tougher mandates, is also subject to severe limitations, Personal income tax rates, that rise with income, are a particular disincentive to high income earners, who have a lead-role to play in the economy. Indirect taxes have an advantage over personal income taxes, in that they are a fixed proportion of spending and so do not have the same disincentive effects for high income earners. More important perhaps, is that they can be imposed as easily on foreign suppliers. But indirect taxes, nevertheless, also raise prices to domestic consumers. By so doing, they reduce the real wages which are the inducement to supply labor.

The unemployment, and other welfare benefits, may well be linked to inflation, so making work (after higher taxes and still higher prices), even less attractive than staying on welfare. If the cost of not working and the rewards for working have both declined, it will reduce the supply of labor to industry further and put upward, rather than downward pressure on real wages, even in a recession. Employment will fall and unemployment increase, as both the demand for, and supply of labor decline.

Whether the firms and their owners are able to achieve such cost recoveries from their customers, suppliers, or workers, will once more depend on the degree of competition they are faced with in the market place. The competition will come from foreign suppliers of goods and services in local and foreign markets and from competition from foreign firms for their capital and labor and also from the competition from the welfare system that reduces the supply of labor to them.

The political appeal of mandates or regulations over tax and spend policies is that it is much more difficult to separate the influence of these exactions from all else that affects living standards. It is harder to blame the government for slow torture than for higher taxes. Budget-stretched governments may be very inclined to mandate cost increases for firms or households, rather than impose taxes, to improve the appearance of the budget. For example, if firms are forced to cover the costs of medical insurance for their employees, that is a mandated cost of employment. The alternative would be for the government to raise taxes to cover the cost of running a national health scheme. Under the mandate, prices will tend to go up and wages down, as firms attempt to recover the higher costs. Under a national health scheme, taxes and government expenditure rise.

The question of whether such mandated costs should be regarded as off or on budget, for the purposes of calculating the fiscal deficit, the government's share of the economy, is bound to be controversial, because of the importance of budget appearances. The first goal would be to measure the costs of the mandates or regulations, and to get the politicians to recognize such costs as equivalent to imposing taxes. In the case of mandated medical insurance schemes, this would be possible. The next goal would be to determine the degree of government involvement in the provision of medical services. The greater it is, the stronger the technical case for putting it on budget. The US Congress Office of the Budget decided that the proposals which the Clinton Administration were making in 1994 for health reform, mandating all employers to make health insurance contributions on behalf of employees, and which also included plans to extend the cover to the unemployed, should be treated as a budget item.

That is, such contributions made by employers should be included in the budget, in the same way that contributions to the social security system are included. Since Americans now spend about 13% of their GDP on what is now classified as privately supplied medical services, this would mean a large increase in the US government's share of GDP, were a Clinton-like health bill to pass into law.

The larger issues are not only about who pays, but the efficiency with which the goods or services are delivered. Furthermore, it makes all the difference if people are allowed to choose the amount they spend on health care, or whether such choices are constrained within some government-controlled service. Such differences will not be revealed in GDP ratios.

Governments have a number of options open to them in dealing with any part of the economy. They can leave a particular market largely alone. For example, by ignoring health and fire and other safety regulations, the demand for restaurant meals or clothing is left largely to market forces. Governments may, however, subsidize some consumers in a particular market, or supply them directly via government agencies and raise taxes or loans for the purpose. The balance of that market would be left to itself, though still very much influenced by government action. The housing market is typically managed like this. A government agency may get so heavily involved in supplying the service, that there is little practical scope for private producers, even if they are not actually disbarred. National health and education schemes may fall into this category. Or, as a further option, the government may mandate contributions to a pension or health scheme, and get more or less involved in setting the standards and scope for privately owned firms to compete for custom. The current debate over health care reform in the USA is about all such possibilities.

The share of government in GDP may be a more or less useful indicator of the efficiency with which resources are being used, and a predictor of economic growth. Clearly it is also necessary to look beyond the budget arithmetic to make good judgments about the influence of governments on the long-term economic prospects of different countries. Quality, as well as quantity, matters for economic performance.

It is exposure to competition from lower-tax and less generous welfare regimes that limits the scope for transfers, taxation and wasteful indulgence of special interests by even the wealthiest countries. High levels of taxation may make it impossible for local firms to survive, and so to provide the employment and income which provide the basis for the taxation that has to be collected to pay for the benefits. This is a reality with which the Scandinavian and European countries, with the most developed welfare systems, have had to try to come to terms. Fortunately, for consumers and taxpayers in these countries, the movement towards freer international trade seems secure enough. Perhaps because it is realized that permitting the free flow of goods from the developing part of the world is an alternative to having to receive a greater in flow of its people.

Measuring the actual growth performance of an economy, relative to what is regarded as its potential growth, will provide important clues about the likely short-term trend in interest, inflation and exchange rates. The following two chapters are concerned with understanding the role played by financial markets and analyzing and predicting their responses to the state of the economy.

1. In Japan in the early Nineties, the investment to GDP ratio was extraordinarily high, about 0.32. In Germany the ratio was 0.21 and in Britain 0.22. (Source International Financial Statistics, International Monetary Fund.)
2. While employment growth in Japan is minimal, with its ageing and declining population and effective restrictions on immigration, measured unemployment remains very low, lower than in the USA.
3. Federal state and local government spending and taxing is included in the calculation.

4. A simple linear regression equation for a sample of 78 countries, that relates the ratio of government expenditure and transfer spending to GDP, to GDP per capita of the countries in the sample, indicates that per capita incomes "explain", according to the R squared or goodness of statistical fit criteria, some 35% of the transfer ratio and 30% of the government expenditure ratio. The 78 country average government expenditure to GDP ratio was 34% in 1985, with Israel having the highest ratio of 68% and Guatemala the lowest of 9.7%. The average ratio of transfer payments to GDP was 8.6%, with Sweden transferring the largest percentage of GDP – some 26.9%. The government expenditure ratio for the USA in 1985 was 37% and the ratio of transfers to GDP, 10.1%. The transfer ratio had increased to 14% by 1992. In 1985 the Japanese government spent the equivalent of 26.6% of GDP while it transferred an extraordinarily low percentage of only 1.7% of GDP. In South Africa the government spent the equivalent of 34.1% of GDP in 1985 – about what would have been predicted by the cross country regression line and 4.8% of GDP on transfers, again very much in line with the norm predicted by incomes per head.

5. The USA, Japan, Germany, France, Britain, Italy and Canada.

CHAPTER EIGHT

SAVINGS AND INVESTMENT AND THE ROLE OF FINANCIAL MARKETS[1]

In the previous chapter, the importance of saving and investment for the economy was stressed. Financial markets link
borrowers and lenders and so determine the rewards for
saving and the minimum returns required of investments.
Financial markets not only help raise capital for investment, but
also keep the score on the performance of investments made in
the past. They inform savers about the value of their accumulated
savings. In other words, they help measure wealth and by so
doing, influence future consumption, as well as investment decisions.

Financial markets have developed rapidly over the past twenty-
five years. This has occurred in response not only to the greater
volume of savings, but also to the much greater freedom with
which savers and their agents, the financial institutions and the
non-financial corporations, have been allowed to move their savings around the markets of the world.

Financial markets connect lenders and borrowers. They allow the acts of saving and investment to become more highly specialized, with corresponding huge gains in the efficiency with which resources are used. It would be a much less productive system that forced all savers to make their own investments and all investors to rely entirely on their own savings. The existence of financial markets, and of financial institutions which play such a big role in them, permits specialized investors to take on more risks.[2] It also permits the specialized savers to avoid them. This encourages these savers to save more, which reduces the cost of financing investments. Any innovation in financial markets which reduces the risks of or improves the rewards for saving, promotes lending and borrowing, saving and investment. Financial institutions, banks, pension funds, etc. are described as *financial intermediaries*. The mediate between the ultimate saver and investors, by borrowing from the one and lending to the other. By so doing, they compete with the direct exchange of money from savers for financial securities issued by borrowers in the market.

It should however be recognized that much of the investment in new capital equipment undertaken by non-financial corporations is financed by the corporations themselves, from their own savings. In most countries, corporate savings are more important than household savings. Non-financial corporations may use part, or the great bulk of their savings, that is, their cash flow from retained profits and depreciation and other allowances, to buy securities issued by banks, the government, or other businesses and households. Credit, provided for households and unincorporated businesses, may account for some of this lending. Cash retained by firms accounts for a typically large proportion of total gross, before depreciation allowances, private savings. In the USA, gross corporate savings have varied from about 44% to as much as 60% of all gross private savings. In other countries such ratios can be higher still with corporate savings, made on behalf of their private shareholders, accounting for the great bulk of all private savings. The mix of savings, whether corporate or household, which differs from country to country, is largely accounted for by differences in tax policies, as will be explained below also. The different tax, and other regulatory treatment, of different financial intermediaries and financial securities, will

107

also explain some of the observed differences in the relative importance of different ways of lending and borrowing,to be observed in different countries.

The proportion of their real income that households save, one way or the other, will depend upon their perceptions of future income, that is to say, their wealth as valued today, that is to say *present valued*. The extent to which they believe that their families, or governments will provide for them in old age, or illness, will also influence decisions to spend or save. Current spending by households can, of course, be financed by borrowing. The wealthier they believe they are, the smaller the proportion of their extra incomes they are likely to put aside for a rainy day and the more they will be inclined to borrow against future income. The more confidence with which they look forward to future employment, and so to their income prospects, as well as to the welfare benefits to which they believe they will be entitled, the fewer risks they will perceive, and so the lower the *discount rate* they will attach to expected income. A lower discount rate means more present value, and so the wealthier they will accordingly feel and act.

It is for reasons such as these that the proportion of measured national income actually consumed may rise or fall, with important consequences for the level of economic activity. The ratio of consumption spending to personal disposable incomes in the USA is illustrated in Figure 3. Since consumption spending in the USA has averaged about 65% of GDP since 1950, the importance of changes in the percentage of disposable income consumed for GDP will be obvious. In short, it does not make much sense to regard GDP as depending on consumption spending, since it largely (65%) measures consumption spending itself. Clearly, if we could predict how much households were going to spend, we would have a very good sense of where the economy was heading. In other words, if we could predict how households feel about their future, we could measure their wealth and how much they would spend. We return to this issue in Chapter 11, where we examine the business cycle in greater depth.

If the national income accountants counted the capital gains or losses of wealth owners in household capital, furniture, carpets and kitchen appliances, etc. as part of investment rather than consumption, some of the observed differences in savings rates across countries would disappear. Adding spending by American households on their own household capital, or on what is defined as durable consumption goods, would raise the ratio of private savings to GDP in the USA from an average of 17 to 26% of GDP between 1950 and 1993. Similarly, any emphasis on personal savings rates, which excludes a recognition of corporate savings, can give a highly misleading impression of what is going on with consumption spending and real savings.

Fig. 3

RATIO OF CONSUMPTION SPENDING TO DISPOSABLE INCOMES

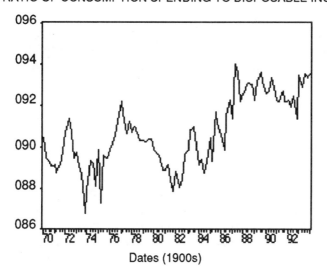

Dates (1900s)

Methods of raising finance.

There are very many different ways of raising capital, from issuing long-term fixed interest contracts, or short-term bills, or accepting a bank overdraft. There are financial contracts which do not promise interest but instead offer a share of profits – in other words equities. There are also contracts that are part fixed interest and part share of profits. Bonds, convertible into shares or fixed income preference shares, are among the infinitely wide range of ways to supply and have access to savings. But the different methods through which lenders and borrowers make contact with each other, are all more or less substitutes for each other. Competition between lenders and borrowers and the financial intermediaries who stand between the ultimate savers and borrowers, will ensure that the prices of, and expected yields from, the variety of financial securities, will be closely related. Competition and expectations about inflation link the yields on short-term securities with those with a very long period before maturity, or those with no fixed redemption date at all. Similarly, the yield in expected dividends from a share, is linked to the alternative, the yield in interest from a bill or a long bond.

Banks and other intermediaries may also package and sell off their own portfolio of loans to buyers in financial markets. This is a version of *securitization*, applied most extensively to mortgage loans and credit card liabilities, held originally, or negotiated first, by a bank. When the banks undertake such sales or activities off their balance sheets, they are no longer intermediaries or principals in the market, but act as agents or brokers for a fee. The risks are passed on to others, though there may be contracts with recourse to the originating banks, or a government agency, that organizes the exercise.

The credit histories of large numbers of borrowers of a particular kind, enable the promoters of the issues to package their separate liabilities together in a security and to calculate the overall probability of default. This enables the promoters to price the security accurately, in order to achieve the expected risk-adjusted returns that will be attractive to the market. Banks traditionally specialized in lending activities where the accurate measurement of default risks was not possible, so providing credit became a matter of judgment. When the market believes that risks can be accurately calculated and priced accordingly, then a direct link between lenders and borrowers which eliminates the financial intermediary, becomes feasible.

As far as regulations permit, participants in financial markets compete with new ways of lending and borrowing and new forms of financial intermediation. The competition widens the market for particular ways of lending and borrowing, by reducing the costs to borrowers and improving the returns to savers and lenders. Such gains in market share and the expansion of the financial markets generally, by encouraging more lending and borrowing, may be achieved in two broad ways. Firstly, financial intermediaries and the institutions of financial markets may achieve greater efficiencies in the services they supply. Modern technologies, computers and electronics have been used to the ultimate advantage of the users of financial markets and institutions. But of greater importance are innovations that improve risk-adjusted returns for savers. Finding more accurate methods to calculate risks, results in new financial instruments being brought to the market that are better suited to particular lenders or borrowers. Better ways of pricing risks more accurately, improve the risk-adjusted rewards for savers and reduce the cost of finance, as the price advantages are competed away. Essentially, reducing risk means to pool the risks that individual borrowers will default, on insurance principles. Reducing risks, through pooling, spreading the dangers of default across individuals, industries, regions, countries and time, is the essence of all financial innovation. This has been the case from the early developments in banking and insurance risks, to the modern mutual funds and securitization.

A larger market for any class of security, i.e. more buyers and sellers, itself helps reduce risks by making the prices realized on the market more stable and predictable, the securities traded therefore becoming more liquid. This means that they can more easily be cashed in without affecting the price. Thin markets are notoriously volatile, irrespective of the underlying fundamentals that would normally influence the value of a security. The discussion of risk and its measurement is taken up again below.

Financial markets and the investment decision

Investors in new capital equipment must at least expect to gather returns that cover the cost of raising fresh cash. This may be from the capital market or financial intermediaries, or it may be the implicit or opportunity cost of utilizing their own savings or the savings of others. Otherwise the investment will not be made.

The expected real returns from investment determine the demand for investment goods. The supply of savings to the financial market is the other blade of the scissors. Interest rates and other related yields for savings, established by the financial markets, indicate simultaneously the reward for savers and the cost of undertaking an investment. This cost, usually expressed as an annual rate of interest, or return, is known as the *cost of capital*. The cost of capital to the potential investor, in physical plant and equipment, may be regarded as the returns available in the market place from similar competing investments of the same risk class, or as the cost to the investor of raising additional finance for such purposes.

Building or buying?

Financial markets establish the cost of capital to potential investors and the rewards for saving, by continuously pricing claims on established assets. By so doing, they signal to potential investors the costs of adding to the stock of real assets. The financial markets provide the answer to the important question: should we build something new or buy something old? When the price of old assets on the market is high, relative to the cost of adding to the stock of assets, the cost of capital will be low and new building, that is, investment generally, is being encouraged. When the markets are down and yields are up, the opposite advice – which is is to invest less – is being given by the market. The price of a financial security reflects the value of the claim it has on a stream of income. A share in a company is a claim on the assets of that company and the income it generates, as is a loan to it. When not otherwise secured by specific assets of the firm, debt holders become shareholders, should the borrower become insolvent. Government bonds are a claim on the taxpayers. Such claims are present valued to establish the price of the asset.

There are a number of equivalent ways of doing the investment arithmetic. One common method is to undertake a *discounted cash flow* calculation. The streams of cash expected from the investment are discounted by the cost of capital to establish an estimated value for the investment. This value is then compared to the estimated cost in money of the same day terms of making the investment. The marginal investment is the one where estimated value is just equal to the known cost of the investment in the real asset, or some financial claim on real assets. Alternatively, the calculation may solve the rate of return, or discount rate, that equalizes the value of the same expected cash stream and the money cost of the investment. If this internal rate of return exceeds the cost of capital, the investment is worth making. For the *marginal investment*, the one just worth making, the internal rate of return is equal to the cost of capital.

Tax rates and the cost of capital

Tax considerations always complicate the investment calculation. Income streams will have to be adjusted for the tax on income. Any subsidies received from government that are related to revenues or output, would be added to the expected income stream. The definition of taxable income itself will be important. Any allowance the tax authorities make for capital consumption or financing charges reduces the quantum of taxable income and so the taxes actually paid out, and thus improves the after-tax cash flows. The cash flows retained after tax are a multiple of the tax rate itself. The higher the tax rate, the greater the saving of tax and so the more valuable will be the allowance.[3]

Usually the tax authorities allow borrowers to deduct the interest they pay from operating profits. They do not, typically, allow firms to make allowance for any costs of using their own equity capital. This makes debt finance appear cheaper than equity finance to the firm. The taxman's logic is that the interest income would be taxed when received by the lender, while the dividend income would not be, and so each type of income would only be taxed once.

But this logic is much abused in practice. Typically, pension and retirement funds, which may hold most of the savings of households in trust for them, largely because there are great tax advantages for households to save this way, are not taxed, or are taxed at much lower rates than households would be on any income, including interest, they receive directly. Taxes are saved until the income is paid out as pensions or annuities. Postponing taxes reduces their burden and *present value*, and so represents taxes saved. But dividend income in the USA, though in few other countries, is also taxed when received by households, though again at different rates (or not at all) when received by retirement funds. In turn, any change in the value of shares owned, is unlikely to be taxed at all. Realized capital gains may be, but then most likely at lower rates than ordinary income. And so firms are encouraged by their owners or their agents the fund managers, to pay interest, for which there is a tax deduction and to make savings, rather than pay cash dividends in order to achieve capital gains for shareholders which are not taxed.

It is tax considerations such as these that explain the composition of savings indicated above. Corporate savings will be substituted for household savings, if they are expected to give superior after tax returns. Again, households will place their savings in pension and other retirement funds rather than in bank deposits if there are tax concessions for doing so. Typically, such contributions are not regarded as part of taxable income, whereas deposits with banks or purchases of shares or unit trusts, are. Thus, an immediate part of the return on savings placed with retirement funds is the tax saved, because taxable income is lower than it would have been without the contribution to the fund. Thus, households in countries where such incentives to save apply, will tend to defer their pay, build up assets in their retirement funds and borrow against such security to finance household goods. They may also be able to deduct their own interest expenses from taxable income, which further encourages borrowing. Home ownership, rather than renting, is often encouraged in this way.

The effective level of taxes on business income and so the effective tax rate is therefore dependent on both the tax rate and the value of the allowances provided. What is taken in the one form, may be returned with advantage in the other. The effective tax rate is not, therefore, simply the percentage of accounting profits actually paid out as taxes. Economists define the effective tax rate as the percentage of *economic income* that is taken in taxes. Economic income means the gain in *consumption power* achieved for the owners of the asset over a period, in the form of cash dividends or their equivalents, and their share of capital gains or losses – that is, the changes in the market value of the assets they own, which are as valuable a source of consumption power as other income.

Accounting profits are often simply defined for purposes of collecting taxes. And so the expenditures deducted from operating profits will typically be those that are allowed, for the purpose, by the tax authorities. These allowances, as indicated, may be greater or less than the economist would regard as appropriate. The economist would define *capital consumption* as the real loss in wealth suffered by the owner of a machine as it gets closer to the end of its useful life. In the case of a machine with an expected economic life of 10 years, the owner would be losing roughly 10% of the savings or wealth tied up in the machine each year. Ideally, such changes in value would be recorded in the second-hand market. This 10% would be part of the cost of owning such capital and have to be recovered in the revenues earned. If the real allowance is not to influence the investment decision, then it should apply consistently across the economy. Economists therefore recommend that the real value of the depreciation allowance should approximate *economic depreciation* as closely as is practically possible. In practice, this would mean linking – *indexing* the amount of any allowance provided, based upon the original money cost of the asset, to the inflation rate.

Often the purpose of the deduction is anything but tax neutrality. It is intended to help influential industries or classes of households. Tax help for those who borrow to buy their own homes is common in many countries. Perhaps the most important scope for favours and influence over investment, is in the treatment of depreciation allowances, making them greater or less than economic depreciation.

Many machines are highly specific and there may be no relevant second-hand market to call upon, to measure economic depreciation. Rough rules of thumb are therefore used to calculate depreciation rates for different categories of plant and equipment. These depreciation rates should be indexed to inflation, but often are not, as the tax authorities and the politicians naturally resist innovations that mean lower taxes, which the public at large would fail to appreciate. Accelerated depreciation allowances or initial investment allowances may be used as a further rough-and-ready way of offsetting the effect inflation has on the value of any depreciation allowance, based on the historic rather than the current costs of plant or equipment. Some companies report replacement cost depreciation, even if there is no tax advantage in doing so. That is, they revalue their assets to market, and take their depreciation allowance off this higher number. They may then be able to justify greater retentions of cash to their shareholders. Industries subject to price control will wish to use replacement cost depreciation to measure higher costs, with which to justify higher prices. By so doing, they may be able to achieve a higher return on their investments.

The way to encourage investments of a particular kind, or in a particular place, is to offer generous allowances, combined with a very high nominal tax rate. The high tax increases the after-tax value of the investment allowance. Considerations of this kind make it important to look beyond the nominal corporate tax rate, when deciding whether a location is favourable or unfavourable to capital. The value of the allowances may more than compensate for what is a high tax rate, only in the symbolic sense. Also of concern to any investor will be the longer term reliability of such allowances. The favours governments give may be as easily taken away. Tax allowances may be as effective in promoting exports as are direct subsidies to exporters. The latter are more obvious are generally disallowed under the fair international trading rules administered by the World Trading Organization (WTO).

Companies may have incomes that fall short of the value of the depreciation allowance to which their investment programs entitle them. This may be because they are just starting up, or expanding rapidly, or making losses. It is usually best, in such cases, to lease, rather than to own the equipment. The lessors then get the tax write-offs that reduce their tax burdens. Competition between firms to lease capital, will ensure that the tax savings are passed on to the lessee. The lease or rental payment will approximate to the true economic costs of using the machinery. If the owner of the capital is to recover all the costs of leasing out the capital, the rental charge will have to cover the opportunity cost of the capital, after taxes, plus economic depreciation. Leasing should not be regarded as a tax dodge, but as a way of presenting all firms using similar capital equipment with the same costs of using the capital, irrespective of whether they are well established, newly established or currently making profits or losses.

The major complications which measuring income gives rise to, especially corporate income, after deductions, have spurred the search for an alternative and simpler tax system that would do away with income taxes, including the tax on corporate income. Many economists would prefer to base all taxes on actual consumption spending. In reality, the tax exemptions typically granted to contributions to pension and other retirement plans in many countries, have already introduced a large element of a consumption-based tax system, in addition to the sales and value-added taxes aimed at actual consumption. Contributions to the approved savings schemes are treated as a deduction from taxable incomes. As with the tax advantaged retirement plans,, when assets are cashed in, they would be treated as taxable consumption, and taxed as would any cash income that was not used to add to the stock of assets held.

The danger with a simpler tax system that meets the economist's criteria of fairness and neutrality, is that it may make taxes easier to collect and by so doing encourage governments to spend more.

Valuing taxes and subsidies

Any tax savings, or penalties, will be priced in by the present value calculation. The value of the investment, after taxes, will be calculated using the income, after taxes, from the next best investment. This means first that the lower is the effective tax rate, the lower the cost of capital, and conversely, the greater the value of the tax-favoured investment, the more of it will be undertaken. Competition in financial markets will equalize the expected after-tax returns from different investments, in real and financial assets. Tax more, and the prices of the disadvantaged financial securities will fall in order to maintain the required market-related returns. Tax less, and prices rise to bring returns down and back into line. In the longer run, the tax-advantaged industry will produce more goods and services, and the industry or sector discouraged by higher taxes will produce less. Then, depending on the international competition, prices of the goods and services would adjust to greater or lesser supply.

Tax reform disturbs what may be a well-established equilibrium and sets up new winners and losers from investments. These possibilities add to business risk and so required returns. There is, therefore, much to be said for the adage that old taxes are good taxes. It is the level of government expenditure that matters, rather than the break-down of individual taxes. All taxes, as well as subsidies, will more or less find their way into the prices of goods, as supply and demand for resources adjust to after-tax rewards. The higher the tax on incomes or goods, the higher the pre-tax incomes are likely to be. Salaries in New York are higher than in Dallas, in large part because taxes and rents are higher in New York.

Tax incidence, that is, who actually pays, depends finally on the ease with which resources can be moved in response to after-tax rewards. Savings are very mobile across different tax regimes and so largely escape above average taxes. But in the long run, so is labor and skilled labor is more mobile than unskilled labor. The owners of buildings or land are the least able to escape with their assets from penal taxes. But buildings have to be maintained, and if the returns from owning them are inadequate to cover maintenance, it becomes a matter of time before the buildings literally disappear from the tax reach. The attempt to identify exactly who is paying the tax, is a task beyond the technology of economics. There are models that address such issues, but no reliable measures.

The most likely method of reducing the tax burden on an economy is to reduce or restrain government spending, not to reform the tax structure. How the government actually goes about collecting the tax, is of a much smaller order of importance for the economy as a whole.

Comparing the price of the old with the cost of the new

Ratio Q[4]

A further direct way of looking at the investment decision is to compare the value of established assets, or claims on them to the cost of reproducing such assets. The cost of buying a representative old asset will be revealed by a stock exchange index, or an index of real estate prices. The average prices of the old assets, as revealed by the index, will have been established by way of the present value calculations indicated above. These average prices, as indicated by the indices, may then be compared to the cost of making such investments. This ratio is called *ratio Q* in economics. An increase or decrease in Q, indicates that investment in new equipment or buildings has become cheaper or more expensive relative to the alternative, which is to buy a stake in an established company or building. A Q ratio of 1, may be regarded as a long run equilibrium condition. When the Q ratio falls below 1, there will be less investment. If so, the stock of assets will decline or grow at a slower rate. There will be less additional capacity and so less competition in the market place, which will improve profit margins and the value of established firms. Q will tend to recover. Similarly, when the Q ratio is above 1, the extra capacity brought onto the market will compete with established assets, reduce profit rates and help bring the value of the firms and buildings back to equilibrium. [5]

Q ratios for housing and equipment in the USA, are presented in Figure 4. As may be seen, house prices and the cost of a newly built housing unit have been closely matched. It should be recognized that the price of an established house includes the value of the land, which may have unique qualities, for which more distant land in the suburbs may not be a very good substitute. The price of land generally should rise with economic growth and greater demands for scarce sites.

As may be seen, the Q ratio for the equipment used by firms for investment has been much more variable than that of housing. The low point for corporate financial strength was in the early Eighties, when established enterprises were selling on the market for about half the cost of re-equipping them with new machinery. They now sell for a 50% premium over replacement cost. In Chapter 11, which focuses on the business cycle, we consider whether these Q ratios can help explain and predict the cycle of investment spending.

Fig. 4

Q RATIOS FOR THE USA

Dates (1900s)

HOUSING — INDUSTRIAL CAPITAL

Another way to measure ratio Q is to divide the market value of a company, or the price of a share, by its net (after debt) book value. Book value represents approximately what has been invested by shareholders in the enterprise, and market value reveals what those investments are worth.[6] Firms with high ratio Qs are being encouraged by the market to grow, and those with low value Qs to shrink, or reorganize themselves. A low Q might also be regarded as an opportunity to buy the share, in the expectation that new management will be put in place to raise market value. It is important for economic growth and the efficiency with which resources are being managed, that, if needs be, established managers should not be able to avoid the challenge of a hostile bid to replace them.

The logic of the share market

Clearly the capital market has a very important role to play in the economy, in signalling for more or less investment growth. The accuracy of the process for valuing established firms and managers of assets, is therefore of considerable significance for society. The logic of the valuation exercise has been indicated above. Value expressed in money-of-the-day terms, is dependent on the stream of after-tax income expected from the assets and the returns from alternative investments. These returns are reflected in the discount rate applied to the expected income stream. For the valuation of shares or buildings for rent that offer no nominal income guarantees, the emphasis is appropriately given to the measurement of expected income.

Valuing fixed income streams, in the absence of risks of default, is a trivial exercise. Determining the domestic, money-of-the-day value of a government bond is simply the present value, discounted at current market rates of interest, of the government-guaranteed interest payments. For such assets, it is expected real income or the income converted into other currencies, that is important. It is the uncertain outlook for inflation and exchange rates that complicates this valuation exercise. These issues are taken up in the following chapter.

But of course only actual income can be observed. Changes in the observed value of assets may well be the result of changes in unobservable expectations, rather than of changes in returns from alternative assets – in other words in the discount rate that will be applied to any particular expected income stream.

In fact, a very large part of the value of shares quoted on the New York Stock Exchange, can be explained by the current flows of dividends and the contemporaneous returns on fixed interest securities. A simple linear regression equation, which includes current dividend flows and interest rates as explanatory or independent variables, explains about 93% of the value of the S&P Composite 500 shares, listed on the New York Stock Exchange[7] In such equations, long-term interest provides a better fit than short. An equation that uses a six-month forward interest rate[8] as the representative of interest rates and the cost of holding shares, does about as well as the one where the rate on the 10-year Treasury Bond represents the return on alternative investments.[9] The results of the model are presented in Figure 9. As may be seen, the market stayed very close to fundamentals between 1973 and 1992, explaining on average 93% of the value of the index. In 1987, before the crash of October 19, when the market lost about 20% of its value, the market was about 34%

Fig. 5

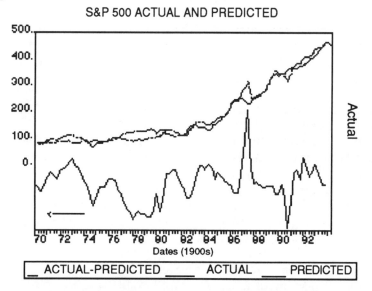

overvalued. In late 1990 and in the period from 1978 to 1980, the market was significantly undervalued according to the model. Such results must be considered an impressive testimony to the rationality of the market in US companies.

It should be recognized that actual dividends are being used in this equation as a proxy for expected dividends or earnings in the valuation procedure. Share owners are attempting to value future rather than current dividends which can change unexpectedly for any number of reasons that will cause the relationship between actual share prices and current dividends and interest rates to change. The economy may speed up or down in a surprising way. Monetary policy and interest rates can always do the unexpected, and taxes, mandates and regulations can all improve or harm corporate prospects. Riots and war can always rock, or even capsize the dividend boat. The results of these equations simply indicate that actual dividend flows have proved a very good proxy for expected dividends, at least in the USA. When the model is estimated using actual dividends, paid a year ahead, the results are only marginally better (the value of shares, in other words, being determined as if dividends to be paid in a years time were known today). If we could find some better way of consistently measuring expected dividends, independently of actual share prices, we could perhaps find a superior valuation model to demonstrate the logic of the share market. Then, on observing share prices changing in response to changing expectations, we could then hope to explain why expectations have changed.

When applying the model with quarterly data[10] and when corporate cash flows from the national income accounts are used in place of dividend flows, the explanatory power of the model falls from 0.93 to 0.82. When national income measures of the gross after-tax profits of all corporations are substituted for dividends, the results are weaker still, with the R squared falling to 0.56. The measures of cash flow, or after-tax profits, taken from the national income accounts, apply to all corporations and not only the S&P 500. This may account for the different results. The correlation between the S&P dividend flows applied in the model, and cash flows and profits as per national income amounts in the USA are however high, being 0.97 and 0.85 respectively.

It should be appreciated that this valuation exercise is more than simply looking at the historic record of share prices to after-tax earnings or dividend ratios, or the earnings or dividend yields which are the reciprocal of the price to earnings and dividend ratios. This equation also explicitly takes into account interest rates and discount rates, to explain share prices.

Market Efficiency

While such a fundamental model of the share market can do very well in explaining the market as a whole, the relationship between the returns of any one share and the market, is not necessarily a strong or a consistent one. There is plenty of scope for superior insights and information about individual securities. Indeed much of the work of financial market analysts is highly specialized and is about individual companies and sectors of the financial markets. But competition to get it right ensures that the mistakes do not have any obvious or persistent pattern to them. The fact that there is no obvious bias to the changes in the prices of securities over time, is a proof of *market efficiency*, or, more fundamentally, of competition in the market. Price changes in financial markets follow something close to a random process. This suggests that the chances of underestimating or overestimating the price tomorrow, or in five minutes time, are about the same. The prices rapidly adjust to new realities and the changes in the

Fig. 6

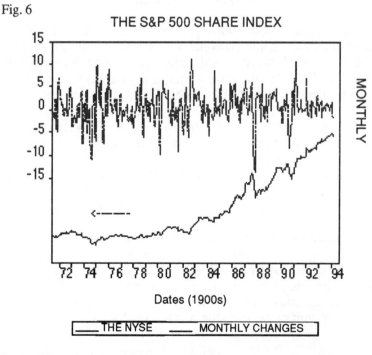

THE S&P 500 SHARE INDEX

MONTHLY

Dates (1900s)

| THE NYSE | MONTHLY CHANGES |

view of the future to which the new facts give rise. Proponents of the efficient market view of financial markets argue that the prices change because the facts change, not because something obvious is persistently disregarded.

The random nature of monthly price changes on the New York Stock Exchange is illustrated in Figure 6.[11]

The ability to recognize error in the pricing of financial securities would provide opportunities to become fabulously rich. Of course a few do succeed in becoming fabulously rich by beating the other participants in the financial markets. If so, they may be very clever or very well informed and their opponents, who made the wrong judgments, who sold or bought from them, very stupid or hopelessly uninformed. Alternatively the lucky few are just that – lucky – and took on enormous risks that paid off.

Statistics measure the probability of a long sequence of heads or tails. They explain that if there are enough coin throwers, a few of them will strike a long winning streak. So it is not a counter-argument to point to a few market magicians who have been able to beat the market over an extended period of time.

The implication of market efficiency is that there are no patterns of prices or returns that repeat themselves. Thus, the work of the *technical analysts* or *chartists*, who attempt to discover and extrapolate past trends, is inconsistent with the notion of efficiency. That so much attention is given to technical analysis, is, itself, perhaps enough to refute the notion of efficiency. But if enough people believe it all, and follow the advice, then even those who do not accept it had better be aware of the consequences – the charts and their magic numbers, the *break outs* and *resistance levels*. This is the only defence of technical analysis that the fundamentalists can accept.

The search for patterns from the past has reached further back into the pricing process. While the changes in returns may be a random walk, the changes in the changes of returns may well have a pattern to them. The market, characteristically, does go through extended periods of greater and lesser *volatility* – when price changes, while not predictable in any way, will move from day to day, or every twenty minutes, by more or less than average. In other words, some days or months are riskier than others. Such knowledge will be recognized by traders in securities, who may have difficulty in avoiding exposure to risks. But it remains moot whether there are methods for recognizing or predicting volatilities that can actually improve realized returns. If there were such methods, this would help reduce risk to the advantage of borrowers.

There are a few other points that should be recognized in the market efficiency debate. There is information of relevance to be gained about the future performance of companies or economies. Gaining such information is not a cost-less task, and the information gatherers will have to be rewarded for their time and competence.[12] In all sectors of the economy there will be different rewards for different abilities and achievement, and the rewards provided for dealing in financial markets are no exception. The market magicians may be no more than exceptionally talented individuals, who receive appropriate rewards that are consistent with their abilities.

The potential rewards for taking on the extra risk and beating the financial markets are of a very high order of magnitude. And achieving great wealth through financial markets, unlike successes in other sectors of the economy, can happen overnight, without any obvious sweat. This is probably why there is so much popular resentment of fortunes made on Wall Street. It is hard for the ordinary man or woman to recognize the relationship between effort and reward, when superior judgments, or just better luck can produce such magnificent rewards so quickly. There is the equivalent of a horse race, or a roulette wheel being spun, every waking moment on every well-developed financial or commodity market. A long-shot can and sometimes does come in. But the proponents of the idea that markets are efficient in processing information, regard the few big winners and losers in the same way as they do the lucky high rollers on the races, or round the roulette wheel. Financial markets can be, and are, used to gamble on, and there will always be some big lucky winners and unlucky losers.

Prices change from day to day, not because of gambling, but

because of the unpredictable nature of the economic forces with which participants in financial markets have to cope. If the economic environment were more stable, financial markets would reflect that underlying stability. There are, perhaps, examples of financial market *bubbles*, when financial markets follow courses of their own that have no connection with economic realities. If so, the return to reality will cause real damage to the economy. But such events, if they occur at all, are few and far between. There may well be good, rational reasons why a market races ahead, and good reasons again as to why it collapses. Fools on the financial markets are usually parted from their money, but there are always a few fools left out there to take advantage of.

Blaming financial markets for instability seems to me like blaming the messenger for the bad news. It would be much more accurate to attribute instability, or volatility on financial markets, to the unpredictability of nature and knowledge. But a large part of the responsibility for instability in these markets, lies with the governments we choose to serve us, or who sometimes impose themselves on us against our will. It is the unpredictability of their actions that is at the heart of the difficulty financial markets have in pricing assets correctly. Prices often reflect the outlook for incomes, dividends, interest rates and inflation over the long run, during which time nature and governments may do any amount of damage to the economy and its ability to generate incomes. The real economy moves slowly in response to a change in the environment. Financial markets move very rapidly in trying to factor all the long-term trends into present values. The benefits of a superior understanding of where the economy is likely to go – and where others, a little while later, will come to think it is heading – can be realized quickly, by appropriate actions taken in financial markets.

Justifying the market

Most of the activity in financial markets in fact consists in the trade in claims on established assets, not the raising of fresh capital through new issues for investment purposes. Financial markets allow individuals to trade such claims and the fact that they wish to do so is surely justification enough for the existence of a market. It is a sign of economic freedom at work when willing buyers and sellers participate in markets. If the market is always efficient, that is the prices are always right, then the only good reason for trading assets is because the circumstances of the saver or fund manager have changed. This, then, calls for a different exposure to risk and the portfolio can be changed accordingly. However, if a further justification for financial markets needs to be given, it is that without a market in what is sometimes described as *secondary* securities, as opposed to *primary* securities, the proceeds of the issue of which go to pay for new equipment, it would be impossible to price the new issues with any accuracy. It would also be impossible to make judgements about the unsuccessful or other use of corporate savings.

The greater the ease with which buyers and sellers can get together and the more of them there are, then the more marketable any assets become. Sales or purchases can be made easily without affecting the market price. These factors in themselves make the prices that are realized more stable and therefore more predictable. A thin market is a very volatile one, irrespective of underlying earnings. Any lesser volatility, which is the result of deeper and more resilient markets, more *liquid* markets, encourages the demand for claims on assets generally and by so doing reduces the cost of raising fresh capital. The punters help bring volume to the market. Well-developed financial markets encourage saving and investment by reducing the risks to which lenders and borrowers are exposed. Lower risks imply lower required returns and so more investment, a larger capital stock and so a more productive labor force earning higher incomes.

Reducing the risks of raising or supplying savings through financial markets, or financial *intermediaries*, encourages firms and governments and households to make greater use of the market as the alternative to doing it all (that is, saving and investing) themselves. However, even when the financial markets are not being used by companies to raise fresh capital, the markets keep the score on the success with which the corporations' own savings are being invested. If the internally generated capital is not being well applied, the market value of the shares and debt of the company will stand at a discount to their book values. Book values indicate the cost to the share and debt holders of actually making the investment. This unsatisfactory (Q) ratio will encourage the search for better management. The directors may be able to do this on their own, or the hostile takeover may be the option chosen. There is a useful role for financial markets in keeping the score.

1. For an introduction to the ideas of modern financial economists and their origins see Peter L. Bernstein, *Capital Ideas: the improbable origins of modern Wall Street,* New York, Free Press, 1992. For a very useful collection of papers that are well designed for the practitioner see Donald H. Chew, Jr. editor, *The New Corporate Finance, Where Theory Meets Practice,* New York, McGraw-Hill, 1993. For an overview from one of the frontiersmen of financial economics see Merton H. Miller, *Financial Innovations and Market Volatility,* Cambridge, Mass. Basil Blackwell, 1991.
2. The concept of risk is discussed further below.
3. Some of these issues were taken up in the discussion of the differences between accountants and economists in Chapter 4.
4. The concept, Tobin's Q, is attributed to James Tobin of Yale University and first appeared in an article written by Tobin in 1969 – *A General Equilibrium Approach to Monetary Policy,* Journal of Money Credit and Banking, Vol. 1, February 1969.
5. The Q ratio may be calculated by dividing an index of prices that represents trends in, for example, the share market or the housing market by an index of the prices of new machinery or newly built houses.
6. The value of the depreciation and other reserves should be added to the book value of the other cash and equity as well as debt capital, invested by the firm to establish the total amount of cash that has been used by the firm.
7. In regression analysis, the power of the equation to explain the variables of interest (in this case share prices) or so-called goodness of the fit of the values generated by the equation, is called R squared. A perfect fit would give an R squared of 1. The closer the predicted to the actual values, the smaller the squared sum of deviations of actual from predicted values the better the fit, the smaller the errors and the higher the R squared. The

errors are squared to prevent negative errors cancelling out positive ones. The actual value of the S&P 500, the values predicted by our equation or model as well as the parts in any month not explained by the equation, and the errors, are all illustrated in Figure 6.

8. That is to say, the rates of interest that the money market expects in six months' time.

9. The model was estimated for monthly data from 1973 to 1992. Changing the data set does not disturb the estimates. For every 1% change in dividend flows the S&P 500 may be expected to gain or lose 22% of its value. Every 1 percentage point move in long rates has on average moved the index by 0.07%.

10. For the period 1973 to 1992 using quarterly data.

11. Share prices whose changes are viewed in Figure 6 are the monthly average of the daily closing prices as represented by the Standard & Poor's Composite Index for the New York Stock Exchange.

12. I hope my readers will be rewarded for reading this and that I shall be suitably rewarded for serving them with relevant information.

CHAPTER NINE

COPING WITH INFLATION, MANAGING RISK

Interest Rates, Real and Nominal, Long and Short
Expected and Actual Inflation

Financial contracts are typically written in money-of-the-day terms. However, what matters to lenders and borrowers is real interest rates, that is, the after-inflation rewards of lending and the costs of borrowing, as well as the real profits and dividends earned from placing savings or capital with business enterprises. This is why *nominal* interest rates rise in line with expected inflation and expected inflation follows and indeed sometimes leads actual inflation. Lenders seek protection from inflation and borrowers competing for their funds are obliged to offer them a reward in interest payments, that is expected to leave something over after inflation. Therefore much of any interest income received is, in effect, a repayment of capital. This makes the taxing of nominal interest income as if it were real income, at the ordinary income tax rates, particularly invidious in an inflationary environment. Such taxes mean that banks have great difficulty in competing for savings with the managers of retirement plans. Retirement plans typically tax withdrawals rather than income. If capital is to be preserved, then only the real component should be consumed and the balance reinvested. Of course there are no guarantees that inflation will turn out as expected. If inflation is unexpectedly high, then lenders lose, but if it turns out to be less than was generally expected, they gain.

The relationship between inflation and long-term interest rates in the USA, is shown in Figure 7. Clearly, higher interest rates followed higher inflation in the USA in the Seventies. When prices were shocked upwards by the oil price increases in 1974, long-term interest rates lagged behind inflation, as they did again in 1979. Inflation fell back again after the oil price shock of 1974. However, as may be seen, the underlying trend in inflation in the USA remained upward.

Fig. 7   INFLATION AND LONG RATES

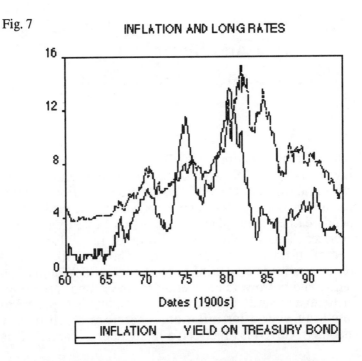

132

The Seventies, in the USA and elsewhere, was a period of rising inflation and slow growth. The escape to freedom from fixed exchange rates made by the USA in the early Seventies, seemed to bring only stagnation and inflation, or what came to be known as *stagflation*. Clearly, the oil price shocks of the Seventies were partly responsible for the stagnation, but the much higher trend to the inflation rate was not inevitable. It was a consequence of highly inflationary monetary policies that were to be reversed in the Eighties.

After the oil price shocks to inflation of 1979, inflation declined sharply, but long-term interest rates remained very high relative to the declining rate of inflation after 1980. Real interest rates remained very high thereafter by comparison with the Sixties and especially the Seventies. Inflation-adjusted interest rates were fairly stable in the Sixties and were very low on average in the Seventies. The relationship between actual inflation and long-term interest rates over the entire period, is somewhat distorted by the oil price shocks of 1974 and 1979, when inflation temporarily increased way above what would have been regarded as its expected level, or underlying trend. The trend, however, was rising and the oil price increases reinforced it.

Ideally one would like to be able to establish a series measuring expected inflation but such expectations are unobservable. It is changes in these expectations that will be the most important influence on long-term interest rates. As indicated, long-term interest rates may be regarded as being set to provide lenders with a real return, over and above maintaining their capital in competition with other forms of lending and borrowing. The difference between this, the presumably more stable real return, and the observed yield on a long-term bond, may be regarded as a good proxy for the expected rate of inflation. A treasury bond carries, as do all fixed interest contracts, the risk of inflation. The actual after-inflation returns provided by US treasury bonds between 1960 and 1965, a highly stable period, averaged 2.76% p.a. This might be regarded as a close proxy for the real, risk-less rate of return in the USA. When 2.76 is deducted from the yield on ten-year US treasury bonds, this amount could be regarded as giving a good sense of expected inflation. The results of this calculation are shown in Figure 8.

This measure of expected inflation seems a highly plausible one. While it may not be accurate to the last decimal point, it does give a very good idea about the trend in inflationary expectations that have driven long-term interest rates up and down. Holders of long-term US treasury bonds, clearly and correctly, did not regard the impact of higher oil and fuel prices in 1974 and 1979 as permanently raising the rate of inflation. Actual inflation moved well ahead of expected inflation. They were expecting inflation to come back to its underlying trend, which however, was also a rising one, as may be seen. As may also be seen, after that it took a long period of much lower actual inflation to cause the bond holders to revise their expectations of inflation downwards. It may also be inferred, from the comparatively large recent differences between long-term interest rates and actual inflation in the USA, that US bond holders in 1994 remain sceptical about the prospects for permanently low inflation.

Fig.8

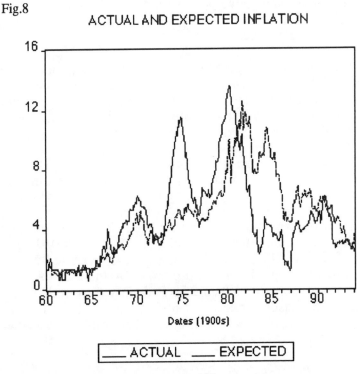

ACTUAL AND EXPECTED INFLATION

Dates (1900s)

___ ACTUAL ___ EXPECTED

The yield curve

The relationship between short-term and longer-term interest rates for securities of the same risk class, for example government securities, is known as the *yield curve* or the *term structure* of interest rates. An example of three yield curves for the USA at different points in time, is illustrated in Figure 9. As may be seen, the yield curve may be upward sloping. That is, short-term rates are below long-term and are downward sloping, or quite flat when long and short rates are close to each other. The yield curve is never stable. It may change its slope or direction from minute to minute. But the relationship between the yields on securities, that differ only by their maturity dates, is an absolutely determinate one if there is competition in the financial markets. The longer-term rates are the average of the expected shorter-term rates over the extended period. Thus, implicit in any yield curve are expectations about interest rates themselves.

When short-term interest rates are expected to rise, long rates will be above short and the yield curve will be positively sloped. If short rates are expected to fall, long-term rates will be above short rates. A simple example will illustrate the forces at work. A company treasurer with surplus cash available for six months is offered the following choice. A 6-month bill at 10% p.a. or a 3-month bill at 12% p.a. After earning interest at the rate of 12% p.a., the funds would have to be reinvested for a further three months at the rate for 3-month money that will be on offer then. Ignoring the complications caused by continuous compounding of interest, should the company treasurer agree to buy the 6-month bill at 10%, rather than the 3-month at 12%, he must be of the view that in three months' time he would be offered less than 8% for his money. If the 3-month rate in three months' time were expected to be higher than 8%, he would do better to invest for three months at a fixed 12% p.a. rate and for a further three months at an expected 8% plus that would provide a return in excess of 10% p.a. There is some equilibrium yield curve, some relationship as between the 3- and 6-month rates in our example, that would make the longer-term rate exactly equal to the average of the quoted short-rate spot and the expected short rates.

Ignoring compounding, the equilibrium condition is approxi-

Fig. 9

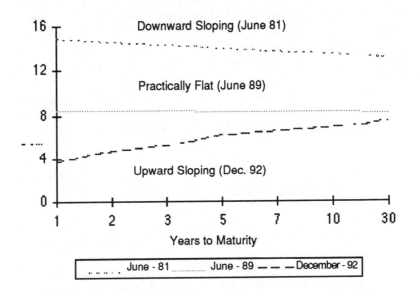

Yield Curve - US Treasury Bonds

Downward Sloping (June 81)

Practically Flat (June 89)

Upward Sloping (Dec. 92)

Years to Maturity

... . June - 81 .... June - 89 — — —December - 92

mately $10 = (12 + x)/2$, where x is the expected rate and so equal to 8%.[1] If x, the implicit forward rate, is not as expected, money will move from the longer to the shorter end, or the other way. Thus the yield curve implicitly reflects interest rate expectations. By taking the 6-month bill and avoiding the 3-month, the treasurer is, in fact, helping to bring the rates into line with his expectations. If the market generally acted as he did, the actual 6-month rate would tend to come down in response to the extra demand and the 3-month rate would go up, to compete with 6-month money.

Such expectations are made explicit in the interest futures markets. For example, it is possible to buy or sell a 3-month US treasury bill (TB) for delivery in three months' time, at a rate of interest negotiated now. Banks can, therefore, without any risk, raise a 6-month deposit to buy a 3-month treasury bill and enter a forward contract to buy a bill for delivery in three months' time. The banks and other *arbitrageurs* would make sure that the forward rate would be very close to the x plus transaction costs above. When such profits are taken, it is called *arbitrage*. To arbitrage away any price differences is simultaneously to buy the same financial security, or commodity, in the cheap market and sell it in the expensive one. The transaction costs help cover the salaries of the dealers, who are continuously watching the markets for such momentary opportunities.

It is always of value to recognize what the market is telling us about inflation and interest rates. The best estimate of changes in inflation are changes in the long-term rate. And the best estimates of changes in short-term rates are to be derived from the yield curve, or the interest rate futures. Before you make up your own mind about inflation and interest rates, find out what the market is thinking.

Inflation and dividends. Equities *vs* bonds

Cash flows and cash dividends will be expected to rise in line with prices generally. The prices and costs that go into the CPI (Consumer Price Index) are the prices charged by business enterprises. The relationship between dividends and prices generally in the USA is indicated in Figure 10. As may be seen, the dividend flows from the index matched the consumer price index very closely until the mid Eighties. Since then, dividends have grown impressively faster than inflation, which largely accounts for the recent strength of the stock exchange.

With higher rates of inflation, the rate of growth of nominal cash flows will rise and the rate of interest, and so the rate at which these cash flows should be discounted, to establish their present value, will also rise. What equity holders gain on the swings of higher inflation, they will tend to lose on the roundabouts of higher interest and discount rates. If inflation turns out exactly as expected, and such expectations are fully reflected in long-term and short-term interest rates, inflation in principle should be neither good or bad for equity holders.

That is to say, if inflation is as expected, real interest rates are unlikely to change and investing in bonds or equities will prove to be very good substitutes for each other. Since they are substitutes, any temporarily good returns from one or the other would be competed away as, for example, firms issued more equities which are relatively cheap to them, and retired more of what would appear as expensive bonds. The suppliers of funds would be moving in the opposite direction to equalize expected returns. Of course, if inflation turns out to be unexpectedly high, other things being equal, bond holders will lose and equity holders gain. Conversely, should inflation fall unexpectedly, then actual returns on bonds will improve relative to those from equities. There is no reason to believe that the estimates of inflation will have an upward or a downward bias to them and there is no obvious reason to prefer equities to bonds or bonds to equities. The expected risk-adjusted returns from all forms of supplying or demanding savings will be the same.

Fig. 10

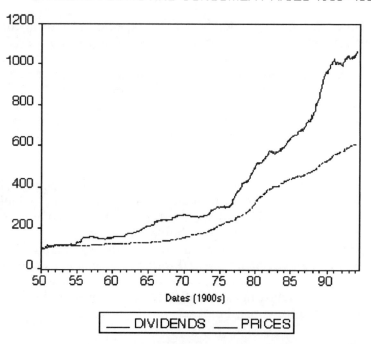

DIVIDEND FLOWS AND CONSUMER PRICES 1950=100

When more inflation is expected, the nominal yield on bonds rises to maintain the real returns that inflation would otherwise take away. The real return on long bonds is the nominal interest rate less the expected rate of inflation. The total expected return from an investment in a representative share index, would be the initial dividend yield, plus the expected rate of growth of dividends. The difference between the long bond rate and the current average dividend yield, provides a measure of the expected growth in dividends. If, for example, the long bond rate is 8% and the average dividend yield 2%, then dividends must grow by at least 6% p.a. on average for the returns from the two types of financial securities to be comparable. Something extra can be added to this growth rate for the extra risk in holding equities.

A treasury bond issued by the government, (that can always print money to pay interest) carries no risk of default and so may be regarded as supplying a default-risk free rate of return. A risk premium would be added to any investment in real or financial assets, where there was some danger of outright failure or disappointment. Lenders would demand compensation for the risk of not receiving interest or dividends, or getting back their capital. And purchasers of real assets would have to expect a higher return to compensate them for the same risks of failure for investing in real assets. A risk premium will be added to the default-free rate to establish the required real returns of lenders and borrowers. At the margin, or in equilibrium, this is one and the same rate. Higher risks and higher returns go together.

The holders, as well as the issuers of bonds, as of all other financial and real assets, are exposed to the risk that inflation will turn out to be less or more than expected. If so, the yields and prices will change to reflect the changing expectations of inflation itself. Investors in the USA, appear to associate higher inflation with more risk generally, for which they expect compensation in the form of higher returns. In the USA, fears of higher inflation push both bond and equity prices lower and yields higher. In South Africa, by contrast, fears of more inflation have been typically good for equities and negative for bonds, as if the market regards inflation itself as favourable for equities. The behaviour of the share market in the USA would appear to provide support for the view that dividends are not expected to keep up with inflation, because higher rates of inflation are associated with a weaker real economy – either that, or because higher rates of inflation make economic policy reactions that much less predictable, to the disadvantage of investors and investment generally. In the Seventies, dividends kept up with inflation, but the share market did not keep pace with dividend flows. It is stagflation, not inflation, that is feared by investors in US equities.

Measuring risk

The riskiness of a particular financial security is usually measured by the variability of the returns it has yielded over some previous extended period. The returns are the sum of the interest and dividend yield, plus the price change, the capital gains or losses, measured over a month, quarter or year. The *standard deviation*[2] of those returns is regarded as the measure of risk. It is higher risks, so measured, that are associated with higher expected returns. Financial securities with a long period to redemption are riskier than short-dated securities. Much more can go wrong or right with them over time, and the price changes reflect this. A long-term treasury bond is riskier than a shorter-term bond and shares are typically riskier than both, as may be seen in Table 1.

The risks, returns and correlations of the returns for bills, bonds and shares in the USA between 1971 and 1992 are presented in Table 1. The returns and risks are calculated on an annual basis using monthly data. The total return for bonds and equities is calculated as the sum of the price change and the dividend, or interest yield. As may be seen, the standard deviations of the returns are quite stable when measured over different time periods, with the returns on bills being much less variable than those of bonds or equities. On average however, it would appear that there is little to choose between bonds and equities in the USA on the risk dimension. Furthermore, the returns on equities and bonds have been strongly and positively correlated. A portfolio of bonds and equities is clearly not a well diversified one. Equities, moreover, have given mostly superior risk-adjusted returns over the different time periods. There is no obvious answer to the issue of precisely how much extra risk should be accepted for the sake of an extra percentage point return. The results for other countries may be very different. In South Africa, both the returns and risks of holding equities have been much higher than bonds.

TABLE 1
A COMPARISON OF RETURNS FOR THE US INVESTOR.

SAMPLE PERIOD 71.01 – 92.12

SECURITY	AVERAGE RETURN % PER ANNUM	RISK (STAND.DEV)
3-MONTH TB	7.35	2.76
10-YEAR T BOND	8.54	13.74
S&P 500	11.41	14.68
INFLATION	5.84	2.97
GOLD	– 7.63	81.7

CORRELATION BETWEEN RETURNS

	3-MONTH	10-Y BOND	S&P 500	GOLD
3-MONTH	1.00			
10-YR T B	– 0.35	1.00		
S&P 500	– 0.072	0.47	1.00	
GOLD	0.006	0.20	0.11	1.00

SAMPLE PERIOD 85.01–92.12

SECURITY	AV. RETURN	RISK
3-MONTH TB	6.31	1.49
10-YEAR TB	14.61	14.38
S&P 500	15.37	11.94
INFLATION	3.76	2.97
GOLD	– 0.57	12.91

CORRELATION OF RETURNS

	3-MONTH TB	10-Y BOND	S&P 500
3-MONTH TB	1.00		
10-YEAR TB		– 0.019	1.00

| S&P 500 | – 0.072 | 0.53 | 1.00 |
| GOLD | – 0.33 | – 0.68 | 0.12 |

SAMPLE PERIOD 90.01 – 92.12

SECURITY	AV. RETURN	RISK
3-MONTH TB	5.46	1.74
10-YEAR T BOND	11.34	5.71
S&P 500	11.75	8.61
INFLATION	4.13	1.14
GOLD	– 3.48	5.04

CORRELATION OF RETURNS.

	3-MONTH TB	10-Y BOND	S&P 500
3-MONTH TB	1.00		
10-YEAR BOND	– 0.50	1.00	
S&P 500	– 0.27	0.83	1.00
GOLD	0.40	– 0.52	– 0.45

Participants in financial markets compete with each other to reconcile expected returns with the expected risks of achieving them. It is such competition that establishes equilibrium and equilibrium relationships, including expected risk/return trade-offs in the financial markets. But actual returns and risks may turn out differently. Such realities may well cause the expected returns and the expected risks associated with any individual security, or class of them, to be reassessed. Risk, the standard deviations of returns and realized returns, can be updated continually. If the risk/return trade-off is to be a meaningful one, there would have to be some stability in the measures as they are updated.

Risks of an individual share are measured by its *beta*. The beta is literally the coefficient on a regression equation that relates the returns from an individual share to the returns from the overall market, as represented by the market index. To calculate the beta for a company quoted on the New York Stock Exchange, the S&P 500 could represent the market. Companies with a beta of greater than one are riskier than the average. When the beta is less than one, the share has less than average risk and it means that for every 1% movement in the index, the price of the individual share has moved by less than 1%. Shares with higher risks or higher betas are predicted to offer higher returns.

A recent comprehensive study by one of the pioneers in this kind of financial economics has rejected the notion that higher betas help predict higher returns.[3] This suggests that the crucial requirement, that this measure of risk be stable over time, is not being met. High betas over one period may be followed by lower betas for the next. Also, the *market model,* as the equation with the celebrated beta is described, must provide an acceptable statistical fit. That is to say, the share must respond to the overall state of the market in a consistent and significant way. Typically, and at best, the market model explains only between 20 and 30% of the returns realized by an individual share. All other factors, not related to the behaviour of the market, explain the remaining 80 to 70%. Thus, in fact, there is every possibility of a share being re-rated over time, so changing the relationship between itself and the market. Some scepticism about the practical usefulness of beta calculations is in order.

These studies also found that the Q ratio of market to book value helped predict returns. That is, companies with relatively low Q ratios (market to book value) tended to offer superior returns. Such results contradict the efficient market hypothesis, and seem to hold even after a *selection bias* is removed and transaction costs are included. Share market data are kept only for companies that survive. The companies that are delisted, because they go broke, or are taken over, are excluded from the sample. This exclusion would bias the results, as only the low-valued companies that survive bankruptcy stay in the sample. The losses from those who fall by the wayside are not recorded, unless, by a painstaking process, they are put back into the sample.

The other important puzzle that financial economists have wrestled with, is the so-called equity premium identified for the USA. That is to say, equities have over the very long run long provided superior risk-adjusted returns to bonds, which should have been priced out by higher equity prices. What may be at work here, is also a selection bias. The equity premium for US investors may reflect the unexpectedly good deal shareholders in the USA have received from the politicians by way of taxes and freedom from burdensome regulation, or expropriation of assets. Shareholders in other countries may not have done so well. The comparison between the returns for equities over bonds should be made for all markets everywhere, over all periods of time, including communist revolutions which involve the expropriation of business assets without compensation. It is these possibilities that may be part of any measured equity premium. Even if the events do not occur, it is unfair to use the advantage of hindsight to judge the insurance premium, in the form of higher realized returns for higher risks, as unnecessary.

Avoiding risk

The most important implication of modern financial economics for portfolio selection, is that the 70 to 80 per cent of the risks, derived from holding an individual share, which are unrelated to the market, can be avoided by holding a well-diversified portfolio. Ideally, this is achieved by combining shares in the portfolio, whose individual returns are not expected to be well-correlated with each other. Again, the stability of such correlations, or *co-variances* of returns, would be very important for such a strategy. Low, or even better, negative co-variances, would allow the portfolio manager to reduce risks without sacrificing much return. By holding a mix of shares that go up or down independently of each other, the returns from the portfolio will approximate to those of the market itself. The further implication of the analysis is that the ideal share portfolio becomes the market itself. Individual investors or fund managers can then select the overall degree of risk to which they prefer to be exposed, by leveraging or gearing up or down. They can reduce leverage by increasing or decreasing the amount of cash they hold in the portfolio, or by borrowing to hold risky shares. Another important implication is that if the risks associated with an individual company, industry or country can be diversified away in a well-chosen portfolio, then the risk premium itself should fall away, to the advantage of the fund raiser. Securities with a long history of returns that are independent of the market, are particularly attractive for their ability to help diversify the portfolio. Gold has some of this character. When the world economy performs well, there is less demand for gold and the gold price under-performs other markets. When economic conditions deteriorate, gold becomes much more attractive. Stagflation was very good for gold. In Table 1 all the relevant investment statistics are presented for different securities and gold.

The search for less risk, without having to trade off returns and a well diversified portfolio, takes fund managers beyond their own borders to other share and asset markets. The market then becomes the world, and the market portfolio a mix of shares that represent the world, rather than the domestic economy. The performance of the Tokyo stock market has been extraordinary, even taking into account the fall back from the dizzy heights of 1989. Between 1960 and 1994 the dollar value of a representative sample of Japanese companies increased some 60 times, compared to a 10 to 15 times increase in the dollar value of the other leading stock exchanges. Finding a new Japan in the emerging markets of the world, is a task that is being actively pursued.

The difficulty with the attempt to achieve a more diversified portfolio offshore, is that the different share markets of the world tend to move together. The different share markets move together because the different economies move to the same, or very similar rhythms. Between January 1990 and December 1992, the simple correlation of monthly price movements, measured in a common currency, on the Tokyo and New York exchanges, was 0.41 and price changes in New York and London were also highly correlated (0.49). The one asset that would have given poor returns, but significant diversification, was gold. The correlation between monthly movements in the price of gold and the New York market over this period was an astonishing – 0.51.

The idea that the ideal portfolio merely replicates the market, has obviously not stopped attempts to beat the market. The game of picking winning shares, or markets, or sectors of them, and winning portfolio managers who promise to beat the market, continues to be played enthusiastically. As I write, the fashion of last year was the emerging markets. However one practical result of the theoretical work done in financial economics, has been the appearance and importance of index-linked funds, which offer convenient access for the smaller investor to a market portfolio. Funds linked to the appropriately weighted global index are also available. Perhaps the most powerful influence of this work is the growing recognition that the performance of the different fund managers has to be evaluated, not only by their returns but by the risks to which they exposed their principals. Furthermore, performance is now typically compared to the returns available from the overall index, or index-linked funds. Just how difficult it is to beat the market, without taking on significantly higher risks, has become apparent. Precisely what mix of risk and return is appropriate for any saver is a matter of tastes and circumstance. Each saver should be aware of the risk involved with all their sources of income. For example, if much of their income is from a safe job, then a more risky asset portfolio would be appropriate. Similarly, it is inappropriate for a pension fund to hold a significant stake in a company upon which the contributors to the fund depend for wages. The markets should be used to diversify risk, unless the saver has some special skill or knowledge with which to value assets. Such individuals are mostly to be found working in financial markets. Individuals who are specialists in some other market should always recognize their amateur, or "punter" status in playing the market.

Futures, derivatives, options and swaps

One of the ways in which financial markets help reduce risks, is by allowing opportunities to buy and sell claims on assets, or commodities, or foreign exchange, at prices agreed upon today for future delivery. Such claims are called futures, or options, or forward contracts. These enable buyers or sellers (producers) of commodities, or borrowers or lenders, to reduce risk. They reduce risk by being absolutely certain of their future costs or revenues. Futures markets extrapolate today's prices and estimates of risk to tomorrow and next year, or as far forward as willing buyers and sellers will agree to. The knowledge of the forces that influence prices today is the same knowledge and understanding that will inform the expectations of prices tomorrow. The most important factor linking prices over time, as quoted on the futures or options market, is the market-determined, expected rate of interest, as indicated by the yield curve. Other influences will be the physical cost of storing and insuring commodities, as well as uncertainty about future supply and demand conditions for the principal security or commodity from which the trade in futures is derived.

By swapping assets and liabilities across the yield curve, the banks are able to match the time maturity of their assets and liabilities more closely. For example, they can make a longer-term fixed-interest deposit for three years with another bank, after borrowing a series of three 1-year deposits from some third bank. The interest rate for the first year would be fixed, and for the final two years rates will be linked to the 1-year deposit rates at the beginning of the second and third years. These future rates, as implicit in the yield curve, together with the known first-year rate, will be expected to average out at a rate of interest that is equivalent to that provided by the 3-year deposit. The bank, therefore, does not expect to gain or lose from such a swap. If interest rates turn out as expected, the transaction would have proved unnecessary. But the bank would want to make such a move to protect itself against the unexpected. If it had taken in too many 3-year fixed deposits and had invested heavily in 1-year bills, any actual decline in the 1-year lending rate would hurt. By swapping, the bank is in effect matching 1-year variable interest loans with 1-year variable interest deposits. The other bank is matching 3-year loans with the 3-year deposit.

Another good example is provided by the futures market in gold. The cost of storing and insuring gold is very low, relative to its value. The future supplies of gold are highly predictable and constitute a very small part of the outstanding holdings of gold. Thus, the future price of gold, as quoted and traded on the futures market, can be observed to be the spot price, the current price, plus the rate at which it is possible for banks or their customers to borrow to hold gold. This is another one of those equilibrium conditions. If the price of gold for forward delivery were greater than the spot price, plus interest, plus storage and insurance costs, banks could borrow cash at today's cost of money and buy, store and insure gold and make a certain profit by delivering the equivalent amount of gold at the agreed time and price. Similarly, the gold mines would store gold and borrow against it rather than dispose of their current output.

Producers of gold, of course, have the same opportunities to sell future output at today's price plus interest. In their case, the gold is still in the ground, but the gold miners will have a good idea about the costs of getting it out. The outlook for the gold mine that makes forward sales is much more certain than for one whose revenues will rise and fall with the gold price.

There are also well-developed markets in share index futures. These markets give shareholders the opportunity to hedge their positions, to lock in a gain or limit a possible loss, should the market decline, without having to buy or sell shares. But others will be doing such sales for them and usually at the lower costs incurred by specialist traders, brokers or arbitrageurs. The equilibrium price of an index future is today's index value, plus the rate of interest, less the expected dividend yield. This is because investors or arbitrageurs can sell the index future, and protect themselves near perfectly by holding the shares that make up the index. In this way, they will neither lose nor win should the share market move in either direction. And when the gaps open up between the value of the index and the shares that make up the index, such gaps will be closed rapidly. When they hold the shares, they will be sacrificing interest income, or incurring borrowing costs, but they will receive a flow of dividends to offset the interest expense. Only the flow of dividends from the shares held will not be known with certainty.

All futures markets provide equivalent opportunities for buyers or sellers, or for borrowers or lenders, to reduce their exposure to the risks of prices or interest rates changing to their disadvantage. Futures markets allow them to hedge their bets by doing business at today's prices for future delivery. The price in the future is almost bound to be different from the spot price plus interest, that is, the forward price negotiated in the past. For example, if the spot price changes over a 3-month period, the forward price negotiated three months ago will not be the same as the spot price after three months. But the chances of its being higher or lower are about the same if markets are efficient. Spot and future prices change together as the market is fed with additional relevant information. The spot price, and its alter ego the forward price, are best estimates, but not necessarily accurate estimates, of where prices will be in the future. They are simply the best estimates you can get.

The futures or options markets, moreover, provide opportunities to speculate that are often not available on the spot market. You could borrow money and buy and store gold and not secure yourself by a forward sale, in the hope that the price of gold will rise faster than the rate of interest. But you would need a bank loan. The futures markets allow participants, including banks, to deal on much smaller margins than is usual in the spot markets. They allow the gearing up of potential gains and losses. In the ordinary old-fashioned way, if banks for example wished to achieve superior returns for their shareholders by exposing themselves to greater risks, they would have to raise deposits expensively from the public to do so. In the futures or swap markets, they can gear up those deposits at risk many times, at low cost. They are able to win or lose a lot very quickly, trying to beat the market. While the futures markets provide ways to hedge bets, these markets also provide new ways for people to lose their money.

The social justification for margin trading in derivatives generally, if one is needed, besides the fact that buyers and sellers participate willingly in such markets, is identical to that previously made to justify gambling in financial markets. That is, by encouraging turnover in derivatives, it improves the market for the underlying physical asset, or primary financial securities. Against this, the argument is made that opportunities to speculate in this way encourage, rather than reduce, volatility. It is hard to see why this should be so. For every speculative and exposed buyer or seller, there is a potential winner or loser on the other side of the contract. The actual gains or losses will cancel out. The losers, however, may be a bank or firm that brings other parties down with them. Some losers are more important to the politicians than others, who may bail them out should it all turn out badly. Losses made in the derivative markets may also give the regulators the pretext to step in to prevent losses, and so profits as well.

How much risk?

Any party who buys or sells for future delivery, without securing the terms of the subsequent sale, or purchase, in the futures market, is speculating. They are betting that the future price will be higher or lower than the spot price, plus interest and storage. The managers of a gold mine, who do not sell forward, are similarly exposing the shareholders to the danger that the gold price may fall.

But shareholders in the mine may well want the management of the mine to accept the risks associated with changes in the gold price. They may have bought shares in the gold mine precisely for this reason. Holding shares in the gold mine is most unlikely to be their only investment – the gold shares may well be held as part of a risk-avoiding strategy. That is, on the expectation that when gold goes up, the prices of other assets they own will go down, and vice versa.

Wealth owners diversify their risks by holding a variety of assets, often through the pension or retirement funds on which they have claims. They invest in a mix of stocks, as well as a mix of bonds and cash and property, and they invest in different countries to diversify their risks further. They therefore diversify through the market, and do not necessarily want the managers of enterprises in which they invest to avoid the risks of prices changing by diversifying for them. They expect to "win some and lose some", and a well hedged position would prevent them winning, as well as losing much. This ability to diversify through the market is the case against conglomerates. These are firms that are a mix of unrelated enterprises engaged, in a diversified way, in different sectors of the economy across the world.

The existence of financial markets allows and encourages firms to specialize, and by so doing to expose themselves to particular risks. Every enterprise is, in fact, an attempt by the entrepreneurs who founded them to beat their own markets. That is, to earn more running their own business than they could do working for someone else. They have to take on more risk in order to hope to do so. They are, by definition, also speculators. If they did not assume greater risk, they would not be able to expect to earn superior returns.

The successful entrepreneur or management team may well prefer to diversify through the enterprise they control than through the services of portfolio managers who may manage their wealth for them. Instead of distributing cash to shareholders from the successful core enterprise, which may have limited prospects of growing further, the managers, or part-owner part-managers, may prefer to invest the cash in non-core activities. However, it will, typically, not only be their own assets or wealth they control, but that of other shareholders also. Clearly, the other non-controlling shareholders would already be likely to have diversified through the market. They do not need an industrial enterprise to do it for them.

Nevertheless, the non-controlling shareholders may recognize that if the founder-entrepreneur, or established management, were allowed to practise their own brand of diversification, they could serve the more diversified enterprise that much better. This could be to the advantage of shareholders generally. They might therefore willingly trade off some unnecessary diversification for higher returns. By forcing managers or owner-managers to stay focused, shareholders may well risk losing their superior talents. A satisfactory trade-off is often made between the shareholders, who would ideally prefer to diversify outside the enterprise, and the founders or managers, who prefer, in their own interests, to reduce their own risks by diversifying through the enterprise they control. This is the case for conglomerates. The trade-off of a less than ideal diversification for more secure management, is revealed in the price of the shares of the diversified company. If the price is unfavourable, the case for breaking up the conglomerate into its more valued parts will become much stronger.

By no means all of the diversified businesses are failures, any more than all highly focused organizations necessarily succeed. For this reason, conglomerates will continue to compete with their more specialized rivals. There is no obviously right way to run a business. Competition in financial markets can be left to decide the mix and how much return has to be sacrificed for lower risks generally. The development of financial markets may well make it harder today to justify diversification through conglomeration than in the past. That is to say, it may be forcing the managers or owner-managers of conglomerates to offer better terms to compete for funds with the mutual fund, or closed-end investment trust, which do not have to get involved in the details.

A business is defined, in part, by the nature of the risks to which it is exposed. The constituency of shareholders will be determined by their attitudes to the risks which the company takes on their behalf. Less risk is not better than more. Risk has to be seen in combination with returns. Higher expected returns can justify higher risks. Shareholders need to be aware of both criteria. It is surely a kind of fraud when risk exposures, as well as risk-reducing strategies taken by managers, are not disclosed to their shareholders. Alternatively, if risks exposures are incompetently managed, this is another of the business risks to which shareholders are exposed. Ordinarily, this is a problem for shareholders and the managers who act for them. Shareholders and depositors with financial institutions have long been regarded as different because of the implications of financial failure for the system as a whole. We will return to this issue in Chapter 12.

1. If interest on interest were to be taken into account the implicit month forward rate would be 7.76% from the formula
x = ((1 + 6months%/200)/(1+3 months%/400) − 1)*400
2. The higher the standard deviation, the greater the dispersion of the observed data about the average value. The more the returns have varied about the long-term average, the higher the standard deviation. Since the higher the average number, the higher will be the absolute value of the standard deviation about the average, standard deviations should be divided by the average for purposes of comparing the riskiness of returns from assets with very different average returns. This summary statistic is known as the *coefficient of variation.*
3. Eugene Fama from the University of Chicago reporting in *the Journal of Finance*, 1992.

CHAPTER TEN

MORE ON EXCHANGE RATES AND TRADE POLICIES

The markets in goods and services, as well as in financial securities, have become increasingly international. Traders and savers are therefore increasingly exposed to the risks of exchange rate changes. It is to such issues that we now turn once more.

Real and nominal exchange rates

The history of the rate of exchange, between the D mark and the US dollar since 1951 is indicated in Figure 11. As may be seen, the currencies of the USA and West Germany were linked closely until the early Seventies. This was achieved by fixed exchange rates. During this period there were also two formal revaluations of the D mark. Fixed exchange rates were abandoned by the USA in 1971 and, as may be seen, the exchange rate, more or less market-determined, has become much more volatile since then. Fixed exchange rates are maintained by a central bank's willingness to sell or buy foreign exchange at a pre-announced price or rate of exchange for foreign currencies. The spread

Fig. 11

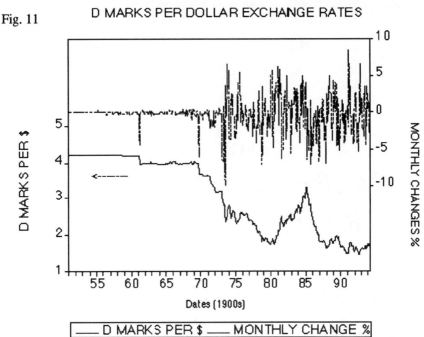

D MARKS PER DOLLAR EXCHANGE RATES

between the price at which it will buy or sell foreign currencies to foreign exchange dealers is usually a very narrow one. The bank holds foreign exchange in reserve for this purpose. But the reserves, in themselves, will never be unlimited. Maintaining fixed exchange rates, therefore, requires that monetary policies follow the lead given by the balance of payments. When the balance of payments is favourable, and the central bank is absorbing foreign exchange presented for sale in the market, in order to prevent such currencies from becoming cheaper, interest rates must be allowed to decline. When this happens, the money supply will tend to grow at a faster rate. If these adjustments are not made in order to encourage more domestic spending, with resulting increases in imports and reductions in exports, the central bank will continue to maintain surpluses in the country's trade with other nations and accumulate reserves, to the displeasure of trading partners. In such circumstances, a formal upward revaluation of the currency, or a devaluation of the currencies of important trading partners, would become inevitable. Currency speculators are capable of forcing such exchange rate adjustment if these rules of the fixed exchange system are flouted.

When the central bank is required to support the domestic currency in the foreign exchange market by supplying foreign exchange (forex) from its reserves, monetary policy must tighten to discourage spending. Otherwise, the central bank will sooner or later run out of reserves and the capacity to borrow foreign exchange. Higher interest rates and slower money supply growth will encourage foreign investment and discourage outflows of capital. The level of imports will fall away, as expenditure generally is discouraged by tighter monetary policy, and local firms will export more as their local markets weaken.

Usually, but as we saw with the case of Europe in 1992, not always, such policies will be consistent with the requirements of the economy generally – the objective of *internal stability* as it is sometimes described. An economy in which demand grows more rapidly than output and incomes, will run into problems with the balance of payments, and out of reserves, unless foreign savings can be borrowed. An economy that is underspending, relative to its potential rate of growth, will tend to run larger balance of payments surpluses and so have lower interest rates, following the balance of payments. This will encourage more demand and capital to flow out. The requirements of the balance of payments, that is, *external and internal* balance, under fixed exchange rates, are normally consistent with each other.

By adapting monetary policy to the signals provided by the balance of payments, local inflation will stay in line with that in the countries with whom fixed exchange rates are being maintained. Any tendency towards faster inflation will make imports more attractive and exports less profitable, so putting pressure on the trading account of balance of payments. By adapting interest rates and money supply growth in response to the balance of payments, exporters and local firms competing with imports remain competitive in international markets. In this way, inflation rates, as well as interest rates in the different countries, remain closely aligned when exchange rates remain fixed. Such alignments are the logical implication of fixed exchange rates.

Providing, and this is a crucial proviso, the rate of exchange is expected to remain unchanged, the offer of higher interest rates in one country will attract capital from other countries. Such flows of funds will support the currency until the higher interest rates work their way through lower levels of spending to lower imports and higher exports. If, on the other hand, the exchange rate is expected to give way, because the higher interest rates that would be necessary to protect the reserves are regarded as politically unacceptable, capital will rush away, making a devaluation more likely. Unless, that is, the country surprises the market by proving itself willing to absorb economic punishment in the form of exceptionally high interest rates. These would need to be maintained for long enough to convince the market of the commitment to maintaining the fixed exchange rate.

The monetary and fiscal authorities in a country without fixed exchange rates can manage interest rates and money supply policies quite independently of the balance of payments. The price of foreign exchange will be adjusted to equalize the actual supply and demand. The central bank may, however, wish to intervene secretly in the foreign exchange market to influence the price. This would be in order to smooth the changes in the exchange rate, as the central bank would describe its actions. This is known as a *dirty float*, compared to a *clean float*, when the central bank does not intervene at all in the forex market.

The monetary policy that is adopted, independent of the balance of payments, will influence the exchange rate, rather than the other way round. The more inflationary the monetary policy, the faster the demand for foreign exchange and everything else is likely to grow. And so the price of dollars and other currencies valued in the domestic currency, is likely to rise in line with the prices of all other goods and services.

The more open the economy is to foreign trade, that is to say, the greater the share of imports and exports in economic activity, the more direct and immediate will be the impact of changes in the foreign exchange rate, and prices generally. The prices of imports and exports, expressed in the local currency, rise more or less immediately when the exchange rate changes. As indicated previously, the smaller the country in population and geography, the more dependent it is likely to be on trade with other countries.

When exchange rates are flexible, the likelihood is that not o will the quoted exchange rates vary from month to month, or day to day, as they adapt to changes in demand and supply, but that what is known as the real exchange rate will change similarly. Real exchange rates change when the exchange rate moves by less, or more, than the difference in inflation between two economies. When the *real exchange rate* appreciates (depreciates), imports or foreign travel become more (less) attractive and exports less (more) profitable. Similarly foreign currency loans become less (more) of a burden to borrowers, and of less value to lenders when the real exchange rate appreciates (depreciates). It is these risks that are avoided when exchanges are made between residents of a common currency area. They share a common currency and therefore an inflation rate, as well as a level of interest rates.

In Figure 12, we show the fluctuations in the nominal and real exchange rate between the dollar and the D mark. As may be seen, changes in the nominal exchange rate seem to initiate changes in the real exchange rate. The exchange rate leads, and the domestic inflation rate will tend to follow, increases in the

Fig.12

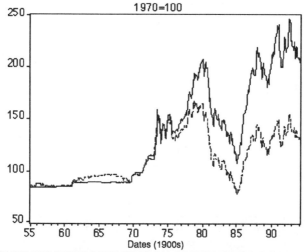

NOMINAL AND REAL EXCHANGE RATES D MARKS PER DOLLAR

HIGHER NUMBERS INDICATE DOLLAR WEAKNESS D MARK STRENGTH

NOMINAL ___ REAL

157

prices of imported and exported goods that react to the exchange rate. The rate of inflation, in turn, will speed up when the exchange rate weakens and slow down when it strengthens.

When the exchange rate changes simply reflect differences in inflation between two currencies, *purchasing power parity* is said to hold. In practice, actual differences in inflation rates have provided a very poor predictor of actual exchange rate movements. In Figure 13, the difference between the actual yen–US dollar exchange rate and purchasing power parity rate, that reflects simply inflation differences between Japan and the USA, is indicated. As may be seen, the actual exchange rate is significantly different from the rate suggested by purchasing power considerations.[1] The overvaluation of the dollar between 1981 and 1985 and the dramatic change thereafter should be noticed. The strength of the US dollar in the early Eighties had much to do with the attractions of the extraordinarily high real interest rates. Countries with very high rates of inflation tend to maintain so-called purchasing power parity, as all prices, including that of foreign exchange, rise rapidly together. In countries with low

Fig. 13

YEN PER US DOLLAR ACTUAL AND PREDICTED BY PURCHASING POWER

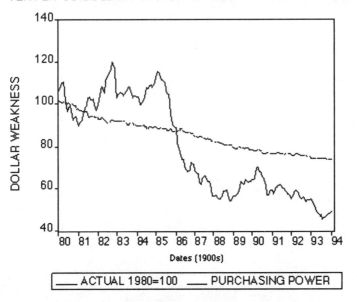

rates of inflation and especially when the dependence on foreign trade is not large, the prices of locally produced goods may well lag behind that of the exchange rate, producing changes in the real exchange rate.

It is not possible to predict that the exchange rate will soon return to what might be regarded as its purchasing power equilibrium or purchasing power parity. The supply of and demand for foreign exchange does not only come from importers and exporters, who are so directly affected by movements in the real exchange rate. As important, or perhaps more important for the foreign exchange market, are capital flows that are undertaken independently of trade flows. These flows are influenced by expected returns over the long run. And these expected returns will be very much influenced by expectations of inflation over the long term. The higher the expected rate of inflation over the long run, the weaker will be the currency in which comparatively higher inflation is expected.

For this reason and because there is so much uncertainty about economic policy in the long term, the forex market behaves like the stock and bond markets. Demands for foreign exchange for purposes of foreign investment, rather than supplies and demands from traders in foreign goods and services, dominate the forex market from day to day. These investors change their minds in response to the news. They are concerned, as are the investors in stocks and bonds, about what may happen to the real value of the assets they own, or could own in one or other country, over the long run. Therefore actual rates of inflation are not necessarily a very good guide to the inflation expected over the longer term. Importers and exporters are buffeted along in the winds of perhaps frequently revised inflationary expectations. Also important will be expectations of tax and other policies that will help determine the returns from foreign investment.

The policy makers in small open economies will be well aware of the impact of the exchange rate on the domestic rate of inflation. The mere suggestion of more inflationary policies to come, can weaken the exchange rate and put upward pressure on inflation itself. For this reason, the authorities may wish to resist such exchange rate weakness and put up interest rates to protect the currency and prove the market wrong. The foreign exchange market, like the market in long-term debt, may, in this way, force a discipline on spending and money supply growth, even though there is no formal commitment to fixed exchange rates.

Insuring against foreign exchange risk

Should the exporters and importers and borrowers and lenders negotiate their contracts in foreign currencies, and should the exchange rate change before the transactions are concluded, they may be better or worse off when the conversion of foreign into domestic money is made. There is a simple way for them to avoid such dangers and opportunities, and that is by locking in the domestic currency value of the transactions. This they are able to do by buying or selling forward foreign exchange at what is the exact equivalent of the current or spot rate of exchange. They would buy foreign exchange if they are importing or repaying a loan, or sell if they are exporting. Delivery would be arranged to coincide with the completion of the contracts.

The difference, premium or discount, between the forward and spot rates, for example, delivery in three months expressed as a percentage per annum of the spot rate, will be equal to the difference in (in this case 3-month) interest rates between the two countries. Thus, it is a matter of indifference in which currency the transaction is concluded. The costs or benefits from borrowing or lending the relatively expensive currency will be exactly off-set by the discount or premium on the forward exchange contract. This equilibrium condition is known as *interest parity*. It allows foreign transactions to be completed in the domestic currency without risk of nominal exchange rate movements, but also with some additional transactions costs. Not all participants in the markets avail themselves of the insurance offered in the foreign exchange market. By exposing themselves to the risks of exchange rate movements, they become, by definition, currency speculators.[2] The currency speculator is betting that the exchange rate will, in fact, move by more than the difference in interest rates between the two currencies.

Similarly, the long-term foreign investor is betting that foreign, as opposed to domestically issued securities, will give superior risk-adjusted returns. The investor in long-dated foreign securities is, by definition, also a currency speculator.

Trade policies

Despite the massive appreciation of the real yen/dollar exchange rate since 1985, Japan has maintained very large surpluses in its trade with the USA, even while trade between the countries has grown substantially. Clearly, there is more to real exchange rates than foreign trade and more to trade, and profits from trade, than inflation differences. Capital flows can also influence exchange rates, seemingly independently of trade flows.

These sustained differences in the purchasing power of different currencies, which are not reflected in exchange rate movements, make it difficult to make meaningful comparisons, using current exchange rates, of GDP or GDP per head across countries. To overcome this difficulty, the World Bank is now using purchasing power-adjusted exchange rates of the kind indicated in Figure 13, to make such calculations. Citizens of less developed countries, with relatively low costs of housing and sometimes food, and with lower tax rates, appear generally better off when the calculation is done this way. Also, the incomes per head of the Japanese, which are the highest in the world when the official exchange rate is used, are reduced by as much as 30% when the purchasing power of the yen is used to make the comparison of the standard of living across countries.

Such considerations, however, make Japan's continued foreign trade surpluses even harder to explain. The inflation rate in Japan has been lower than in the USA, and the exchange rate has appreciated by more than this difference, making exports less profitable and imports more attractive. Also, despite lower real import costs, Japan remains a comparatively expensive country to live in. That is to say, Japanese firms have remained internationally competitive, despite a very strong real exchange rate and a high cost of living which is presumably also reflected in wage and salary levels and in wage costs to employers. The Japanese firms, to remain profitable, must have been able to retain at least part of the impressive gains in productivity made by Japanese industrial workers. That is, not all the gains are necessarily passed on in higher wages or lower prices.

Part of the difficulty in interpreting these contradictions lies with the calculation of the inflation rate itself. If the weights applied to the calculation of the CPI differ, as they do, from country to country, because the patterns of consumption are different, then price indices and inflation rates across countries, are not directly comparable. Thus the notion of purchasing power parity applies directly only to goods that are traded internationally. For example, the warehouse price of copper is identical, adjusted for distance from the copper mines, in New York, London and Tokyo, whether the price is calculated in yen, pounds sterling or dollars. If not, copper will be moved from one market to the other. The price of an apartment in the best part of these cities will be very different. Not all goods and services, including especially, the services that incorporate high rentals for land, for example a meal in a restaurant or a night in a hotel, can be traded internationally, to eliminate price differences across countries. But tourists and the providers of services respond to differences in such costs and prices. They travel to, and locate, in the less expensive cities and countries, so affecting the balance of trade in non-factor services and help to move exchange rates closer to purchasing power parity.

The existence of any large gaps between the prices of domestically produced manufactured goods sold at home and elsewhere is worth closer examination. Such gaps may be the result of large differences in the costs of distribution, which are also associated with land costs and rentals. By all accounts, the productivity of blue collar workers in Japan has increased much faster than that of white collar workers or workers employed in distribution. This is because the numerous Mamma and Papa shops in Japan have enjoyed protection against competition for political reasons. Higher retail prices in Japan can be associated, in part, with these higher costs.

The price gaps between the home and foreign market prices of similar goods would ordinarily be exploited by foreign firms in the absence of barriers to trade. The USA, in disputes over trade policies with Japan, has pointed to large price differences for particular manufactured goods sold in Japan and elsewhere, and regards these as *prima facie* evidence of non tariff barriers to imports into Japan. The USA has tried to impose numerical targets on US imports into Japan as a solution to the apparent unfairness of Japanese trading practices. Being able to sustain relatively high prices charged to domestic consumers, by keeping out competition from imports, can provide a source of profits for the local firms which can then be retained and invested by them. Industrial policies may, in this way, force savings from consumers and make producers profitable enough to facilitate a continued high rate of investment that maintains international competitiveness in the face of adverse movements in real exchange rates.

Consumers lose out when such industrial policies are applied, as they appear to have done in Japan and in some of the other fast growing South-East Asian countries, for example Singapore and South Korea. Such industrial policies promote investment at the expense of consumption. But foreign trade, at least between developed countries, is a two-way street, as the Japanese have been forced to recognize. If local politics permit, developing countries are likely to enjoy more latitude to enforce savings with which to build an industrial structure.

The secret of success, even when the political will and opportunity to force down consumption is available, is for the savings to be invested in sectors of the economy where export successes are being achieved. Protection in the home market can be made conditional on export achievements. But once the successful firms become a competitive threat to manufacturers in the developed countries, access to the markets of the major industrial countries will be conditional on adopting what are regarded as fair trading policies. If so, consumers will then come into their own.

The successful application of top-down policies, successful in the sense that while consumers lose out now, they get more later, is the exception rather than the rule. More usually, savings are forced from powerless consumers and used for arms and palaces, or to support an elite, or to make prestigious investments in industries that have no chance of competing internationally.

Developments since the Second World War in Russia, China and India and North Korea, and in Japan and Germany before 1945, provide terrible examples of this kind of abuse. There can be little doubt, however, that the phenomenal economic success of Japan over the past 40 years has inspired emulation of and cooperation with Japan, which has helped make South-East Asia the fastest growing region of the world.

1. The average under-valuation of the US dollar *vs.* the yen over this period was 14.8%. The maximum over-valuation was 22.3% and the maximum under-valuation as much as 53%.

2. It is the business of specialist currency traders to supply or demand currencies for forward delivery. They are on the constant lookout for gaps in the money and foreign exchange market, that will provide them with a riskiness profit. When the gaps are found they are closed immediately. The riskiness profit is any difference between the cost of borrowing or rewards from lending the one currency rather than the other, that is, any gap that might emerge between short-term interest rates in the two countries and the discount or premium of the forward over the spot rate of exchange, which may also be expressed as an annual interest rate. A simple example will illustrate a divergence from interest parity. Assume a one-year bank bill yielded (or could be issued at) 5% in London and 3% in New York. Also that the pound for delivery in one year's time was available at a discount of 1.0% to the US dollar. Then a bank could borrow at 3% in New York, lend at 5% in London, gain an extra 2% and lose only 1% on the conversion back into US dollars at the end of the year. There is a certain 1% to be made on every such transaction. Such opportunities will attract enough such transactions to raise the forward discount, and or narrow the interest spread to restore interest parity.

CHAPTER ELEVEN

TAKING THE PULSE: DIAGNOSING THE BUSINESS CYCLE

Having discussed the economic potential of nations and some of the fundamentals of financial and exchange markets, we now turn to a discussion of the business cycle. The financial markets and exchange markets respond to pressures on the economy's capacity to produce more goods and services in predictable ways. If we can judge the long-run potential of the economy and measure and recognize the current state of the economy accurately, we will have a very good idea what to expect of financial and exchange markets and of the real economy itself. Such knowledge is obviously very useful to all business and not only for those that directly participate in the financial and exchange markets.

The long and the short run

A good sense of the ups and downs of the business cycle may be gathered by comparing the growth of the economy, as measured by GDP, to its average growth over some longer term. In Figure 21, the growth of the US GDP is measured in two ways and is compared to the average growth of 2.9% p.a. achieved between 1960 and 1992. The phases of faster and slower growth can then be identified.

Fig. 14

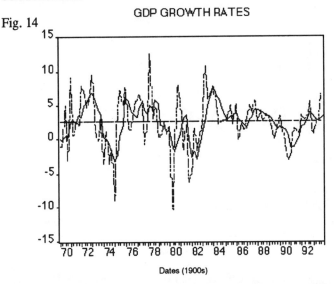

GDP GROWTH RATES

Dates (1900s)

Characteristically, as indicated in the figure for growth in the USA, an economy grows in phases of accelerating and decelerating growth. If the economy picked up pace last quarter, then the economy is likely to maintain its upward momentum this quarter. Similarly, a slowdown in activity is likely to be prolonged. As may be seen, these phases of faster or slower growth are by no means regular. The upswings may be steady and extended and the downswings, the phases of declining or much below average growth rates, of mercifully limited duration. The next time round, the upswing may be much shorter and the economy may continue to slow down for much longer before it turns upwards again. All that can be known in advance, is that the economy will gather momentum in one or other direction for a more greatly or less extended period of time.

The task for the economic forecaster is to identify and, better still, predict the turning points in the economic cycle. As may be seen in Figure 14, in 1973, 1981, 1983 and 1987, growth rates, while at a peak, then began to slow down and continued to do so until the bottom, or trough, of the cycle was reached as in 1975, 1983, and 1990. That is, the period when growth rates, though low by comparison with the average, stop declining and accelerate until the next peak is climbed.

Such knowledge would help forewarn those exposed to the dangers of over- or underestimating the economic outlook. It would help them to avoid spending too much, or taking on additional risks, when the economy is running out of steam near the end of a boom. It would also help prevent firms or households from postponing important decisions, when the economy is in the process of lifting itself out of the trough. This is the best possible time to become committed to new projects and equipment, because supply prices, for example of houses or machinery, are low and competitors are unlikely to be as well placed to take advantage of the upturn in demand. Clearly, recognizing or predicting the turning points would help governments know when to apply more of the brake or accelerator.

The precise state of the economy, however, is far easier to determine some time after the event than while events are actually taking place. The weather, good or bad, may have temporary effects on production and sales. Industrial action may also disturb the picture temporarily. It is no easy matter to separate out, as well as to interpret, a firm underlying trend, the data for which take time to collect and disseminate, from the latest reports on the economy. Making sense of the latest information often requires the use of statistical techniques that average and smooth the actual numbers. An example would be attempting to take out the purely seasonal influences, like summer sales, or winter disruptions. But smoothing and averaging reduces the importance of the latest numbers. Such a bias may cause observers to miss something new and important going on. But if any sense of the numbers is to be made, smoothing and averaging is unavoidable. This means that only time can tell whether what appears to be a change in the trend will be sustained – by which time the mistake of underestimating or overestimating the state of health of the economy may have been made.

The problems of knowing exactly where we stand is illustrated by the pattern of quarterly US GDP growth rates shown in Figure 14. The statistic for growth most commonly referred to, is that of changes in the seasonally adjusted GDP from one quarter to the next, converted into an annual equivalent. That is to say, it is presumed that the economy will grow at the same rate it did from one quarter to the next one, for a year. As may be seen, these annual growth rates vary significantly from quarter to quarter, making precise interpretation of the underlying trend difficult. The problem, as shown, may be addressed by smoothing the data. GDP this quarter, may instead be compared to GDP in the same quarter of the previous year, for the purposes of calculating growth. A clearer view of the trend emerges when quarterly growth data are smoothed. But, as may also be seen, the underlying trends are likely to be least clear when the economy reaches historically determined turning points, as for example during 1991 in the USA.

For the economics historian deciding what happened, or the economics theorist attempting to explain why it happened, well after the event itself, this does not matter at all. For the business economists and the managers they advise, who are obliged to decide exactly how strong the economy is today in order to predict where it will be tomorrow, these are matters of the greatest concern. The state of the economy is also of great concern to voters and politicians. The 1992 US presidential election was decided, in large part, as a result of dissatisfaction with the state of the economy. Had the voters been convinced that the economic expansion was well under way by November 1992, as the economists and statisticians now are, the election result, which saw the defeat of the incumbent, Mr Bush, by Mr Clinton, might have been very different.

Many other important pieces of information about the state of the economy are used to help decide whether it has in fact turned a particular corner, or is still going in some established direction. For example, industrial production, retail sales and employment and unemployment claims are among the literally hundreds of series, updated monthly and quarterly, sometimes even on a weekly basis, that are examined closely by economy watchers. Nevertheless, as may be seen in Figures 15, 16 and 17, it is not

Fig. 15

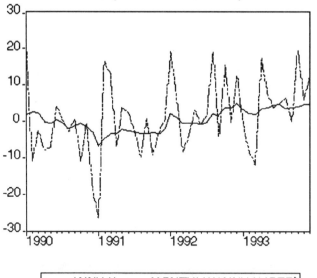

GROWTH IN REAL (INFLATION ADJUSTED) RETAIL SALES

——— ANNUAL ——— MONTHLY(ANNUALISED)

Fig. 16

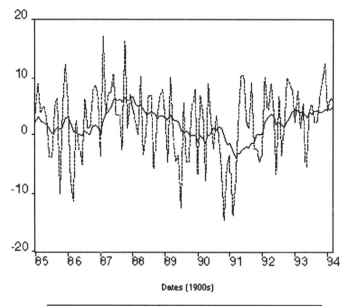

GROWTH IN INDUSTRIAL PRODUCTION

Dates (1900s)

——— ANNUAL ——— MONTHLY (ANNUALISED)

169

Fig. 17

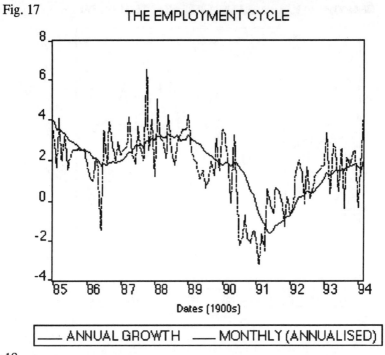

THE EMPLOYMENT CYCLE

Dates (1900s)

—— ANNUAL GROWTH —— MONTHLY (ANNUALISED)

Fig. 18

GROWTH IN US EMPLOYMENT CALCULATED IN DECEMBER 1991

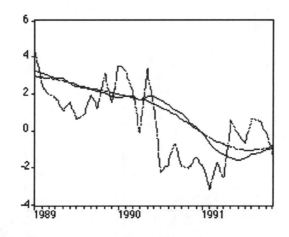

YEAR ON YEAR —— MONTHLY (ANNUALISED) —— YEAR ON YEAR SMOOTHED easy to draw firm conclusions about the state of retailing, or industry or employment in the USA on a monthly basis. Deciding on the precise stage of the retail cycle is particularly difficult. The smoothed cycle of industrial production (Figure 16) and especially employment (Figure 17) seems to reveal a much more regular pattern.

But if we took ourselves back to November 1991, and had to work with the data available then, even the employment cycle would not have been at all clear, as may be seen in Figure 18. It would have been a bold economist who would have gone on line, in December 1991, with the news that, despite four months of declining growth rates in the monthly data, a recovery in employment, and so in the economy generally, was indeed under way, as indeed it was. The smoothed cycle was saying as much, but another weak month would have been enough to have reversed the positive trend.

Much of the work of economists in business and government, consists in reading these and other entrails of the economy, in the attempt to interpret, and better still predict, its state of health. The Holy Grail would be the discovery of a leading indicator that led the economy, as measured by GDP, by a consistently reliable six months. The electronic revolution has improved enormously the power to collect and disseminate information about the economy. This has helped to close the gaps and lags in recognizing what is going on. But leading indicators have not always proved to be reliable or firm measures of the stage of the economic cycle, or of showing when the economy is about to turn up or down. The trouble is that no two cycles are exactly alike.

Explaining the cycle

Despite the measurement and interpretation problems, there is a business cycle out there, even if the only regularity is that a trend, once established, persists for some extended period of time. The reason for such persistence is, perhaps, fairly obvious. If consumers go out and spend more, retailers will sell more and their inventories, or stock in trade, will be depleted. So they will order more from manufacturers, who will work more overtime,

Fig. 19

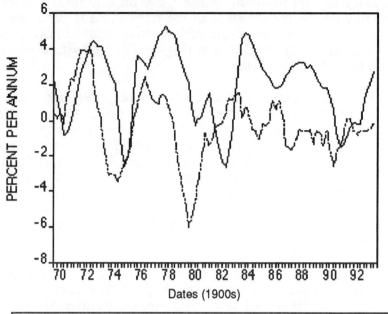

GROWTH IN EMPLOYMENT AND REAL WAGES

Dates (1900s)

_____ EMPLOYMENT GROWTH _____ CHANGE IN REAL WAGES

hire more labor; and so workers will earn more and so spend more, so reinforcing good feelings and good results. Of course, when for one reason or another, the economy then slows down, deterioration sets in for similar reasons. Sales disappoint, inventories increase, orders decline, fewer people are hired, and so on.

Wages and employment

One of the more important cycles is that of real wages. Wage incomes account for the great bulk of all incomes. In the USA, of all the incomes received by American households between 1985 and 1992, 65%, on average, was in the form of wages and salaries and other employment benefits. The balance was income from property and transfers from government. In the USA, the real wage cycle leads the employment cycle in a highly reliable way, as may be seen in Figure 26.

Employment itself moves in line with or lags a little behind the

172

GDP cycle. As the economy improves, and competition for labor increases, real wages respond first, and employment later. Similarly, as the economy weakens, firms and their employees adjust wages ahead of lay-offs. Thus the real wage cycle may be regarded as a useful leading indicator for the economy generally. The changes in real money wages[1] help the economic system adjust to changes in supply and demand conditions, and to stabilize employment. Clearly, real wages are not inflexible, as is sometimes claimed.

The issue is rather about how they might be made more flexible, in the interest of keeping people in jobs when the cycle turns down. Unemployment benefits and minimum wage legislation, as well as the bargaining strength of trade unions, help restrict the flexibility of nominal wages, at least in the downward direction. Recognition of such inflexibility helped promote the idea that the only effective way to get real wages down to promote employment, was to get prices up. We will return to the links between inflation and GDP and employment growth.

Lending and borrowing

The business cycle has its origins in the decisions that firms and households make to save or borrow more or less. Borrowing and lending break the direct dependence of current spending on current income. Borrowing and lending, saving or dissaving, enable potential spenders, households and firms, as well as government agencies, to take the longer view. They can spend today in expectation of incomes available later – next year or even much further ahead. If we had no financial and credit markets, if we could not lend and borrow, the economy would be much less productive but it would also be less variable. The decision to save and plant the seed corn would be taken by the same person. Any inventor, (or prospector) with a discovery that could change the world, would have no alternative but to go out and try to prove it, using their own savings. There would be no adjustment problem, because the decisions to save and invest would all be taken by the same economic actor. There would be no problem coordinating the savings and investment decisions of those who spend less than their incomes and those who spend more.

In a developed economy, decisions to save and invest, or to save less and consume more, have to be coordinated, not only by changes in interest rates but by changes in the rate of growth. The business cycle may be regarded as part of the price we pay for specialization of economic functions, without which improved living standards would be impossible.

Looking ahead takes imagination and confidence. Convincing suppliers of savings – the managers of banks or portfolios, who act as the agents of the ultimate savers, or perhaps some venture capitalists – to place confidence in a firm or household, even with the best-laid plans and income prospects, is rarely easy. It is often necessary to provide the suppliers of funds with comfort, that is security, by demonstrating adequate current income or savings, to cover some of the risks to which the borrower and lender will be exposed, or by showing a good credit record. In this way, the future is bound inevitably to the past.

The importance of cash flows

The uncertainties associated with the future also make firms dependent to an important degree on their own earnings to finance their spending decisions. This is why successful small firms grow mostly by reinvesting their profits. The main source of additional capital for large firms will also, typically, be their own savings, in the form of depreciation reserves and undistributed profits. Even in the USA, with its highly developed capital market and relative tolerance of debt, as well as a tax system that allows borrowers to deduct the interest expenses of borrowed capital and not the opportunity cost of equity capital, corporate savings are far more important than personal savings. Over the past ten years corporate savings have been equivalent to over 65%, on average, of private investment spending. In Figure 20, the corporate cash flow and investment growth cycles for the USA are superimposed. The cycles are clearly linked. Improvements in cash flow lead investment demand, though the timing lags and investment reactions to cash flow are by no means consistent or proportional. The exception was in 1985, when cash flows were on the way to recovery but didn't make it,

Fig. 20

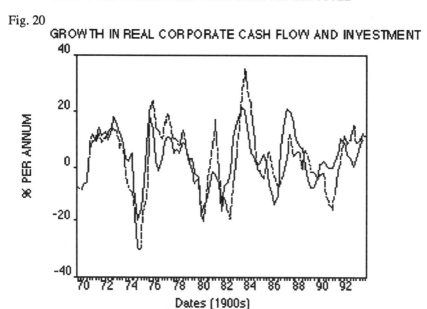

GROWTH IN REAL CORPORATE CASH FLOW AND INVESTMENT

and so investment failed to respond. It should however be recognized that the upturn in the cycle in 1985 meant only that cash flows had begun to decline at a slower rate. Even at the peak of the cash flow cycle in 1985, profits were still lower than a year before. In 1990, a limited recovery in cash flows to corporations also seemed to do little for investment growth or the economy. It has taken the sustained improvement in cash flows in 1992 and 1993 to put US investment growth on a strong upward tack. If anything, it would appear that investment growth leads, rather than follows, changes in Q. It would appear, therefore, that the cash flow cycle leads investment, and cash flows lead the stock market, and so changes in ratio Q.

Financial ratios and balance sheets

The pressures on households and firms intensify when income growth falls behind spending growth. When earnings move ahead of spending, this clearly encourages more spending. Similarly, the corporate sector in general may have difficulty in maintaining expansion unless supported by improved bottom lines or, rather, cash flows. These pressures on all households, firms and the state, when it raises capital, may be indicated by ratios of debt to current income. However, it should be appreciated that it is not only wages and salaries, or the current income of firms, that matter for balance sheets and financial strength. Changes in the value of assets and liabilities, real estate, equities, as well as corporate and government bonds, are also important for financial strength or weakness.

Asset prices will change when potential investors become more or less confident about future earnings prospects. But whatever their cause, such changes have effects. The change in value adds or subtracts from wealth, and so influences the willingness to spend and lend, and the ability of wealth owners and firms to borrow. But these higher or lower prices, relative to some norm, become very vulnerable to a reversal, should the expected change in earnings and cash flows not materialize. Sooner or later, the income realities will reassert themselves. Actual earnings and dividends are highly relevant in establishing or confirming the value of shares over the long run. But regression to some average or normal relationship between the prices of assets, including share prices and their current earnings, may well take a long time. Timing, as they say, is everything, but is never obvious until after the event. Moreover, to complicate the usefulness of the notion of a regression to some norm (the idea, that is, that markets are under- or over-valued by historic standards), is the possibility that economies may permanently change their performance, for the better or the worse. The asset markets might be anticipating such permanent changes, in which case a new norm will have been established. Given enough time, this too will become apparent from the actual growth in earnings and income.

Capital gains or losses are properly regarded as income, as they represent as useful a source of purchasing power as any other source of income. They are conventionally included as such in the measures of financial market performance, but are excluded in the calculation of national income or GDP. The decision not to spend the extra income received by owners when asset prices rise, is also as much a decision to save as is putting aside part of a salary into a retirement plan. Thus, when the prices of assets

176

are rising, including when the equity in owner-occupied homes, market value less mortgage, is increasing in value, households are encouraged to spend more of their wage and salary incomes, or to borrow more. This extra spending will appear to the national income accountants as a reduction in savings. In reality, true savings may have increased significantly.

Integrating the different sectors of the economy

In order to understand the decisions of households and firms to spend, save and borrow, we clearly need to look closely at the balance sheets of firms and households, rather than only at current flows of wages, salaries and other sources of income, including the interest and dividends they receive. A further item on the liabilities side of the household budget, is government debt. The households have to pay the mortgage that is, taxes will be levied to pay the interest. Government debts are their liabilities.

Households, as shareholders, or indirectly as members of retirement plans or pension schemes, own the corporations. The officers of corporations manage resources on behalf of the households and the success they achieve or, more particularly, the success they are expected to achieve, is reflected in share and corporate bond prices. The managers of corporations act for their owners when they undertake savings and investment decisions. Personal, corporate and government savings are highly substitutable. In different countries you may find proportionately more of the one than the other. But such differences will be accounted for by differences in the tax and legal frameworks that provide more or less encouragement for business organizations to establish themselves as corporations, to retain earnings rather than pay them out, or to pay dividends on equity capital, or interest on debts. Thus the distinctions made between the households, firms and the government sector can obscure the reality of their wholeness. The households are the principals and the corporate and government officials their agents.

Booms and recessions. Some asymmetrical relationships

The problem, or rather the reality, is that sooner or later any boom, that is to say a period when recorded growth rates are very high relative to their average, will be killed off, because of the dependence of all kinds of spending on current incomes. Again, this is simply the economic problem restated. It is the inability to produce more output and incomes that sets the limits to, or constrains, growth. The changes in interest, wage and exchange rates, as well as of the prices of shares and real assets, and of goods and services themselves, have cycles of their own, that sometimes lead and sometimes follow the movements in real output and incomes. These changes are part of the process of adjustment of actual demand to limited supplies. Or, in recessions, it is the way in which temporarily insufficient demand is being encouraged to absorb potential supply.

It is perhaps more obvious why the limits to growth will sooner or later slow down the economy than why a recovery must follow a recession. Recessions also tend to end, sooner or later, when appropriate adjustments to harsh realities have been made. That is, a recovery occurs sooner or later, after the debt ratios and the balance sheets of the households, firms and government agencies have been restored to strength. This relative strength is achieved through the realization of savings and the benefits of the greater efficiencies that "caused" the recession. Lower interest, wage and exchange rates may also provide encouragement for more employment, output and spending. But absolutely necessary, in order that households and firms should wish to spend more, is a recovery of confidence in their economic prospects. Something must happen to make the horse want to drink the water, and it usually does. In the case of booms, the water eventually dries up. With recovery from recession, purely psychological factors such as the will, become very important. Without a recovery in confidence, an economy can continue to implode: less being spent and less earned and so less spent.

As part of a long process of economic decline, capital and skills may be easily and continually withdrawn and transferred away from an economy in distress. Thus there is always the possibility of a recession becoming a melt-down, which makes any firm indication of recovery back to the norm very welcome. There are any number of examples of what may be described as economic system failure, when recessions turn into something worse, and when an economy fails to recover and achieve previous levels of output and growth rates for an extended period of time. The export of savings, as well as their owners, from some Latin American countries through the Seventies and Eighties, as also from South Africa between 1985 and 1992, occurred on a scale sufficient to make economic growth impossible. There are many other examples of a shrinking economy in which, if the economy recovers, it does so about a falling trend which provides little encouragement. The USA during the great depression of 1930–1939, provided a very important example of an economic system failure. It took until 1939 for US GDP to recover to levels previously attained in 1929. This system failure had a profound influence on the way economists came to think about the economy. It made economists think about insufficient demand, rather than supply as the problem. The economics profession has been dominated by American and, to a declining extent, British economists and so the cases that receive deepest analysis are naturally taken from their own economies.

As indicated, the economic or business cycle is fundamentally the result of households and firms saving less or more of their current income. Something – some *shock* as economists would say – sets this process off. It may be the result of firms or households coming to have greater or lesser confidence in their economic prospects. The changing impression given by governments may be very important in inspiring or undermining confidence. The shock may also come from new technologies, or new discoveries that stimulate more investment and borrowing. The shocks may emanate from abroad, in the form of higher or lower prices for exports or imported raw materials, and especially for energy. The oil price shocks of 1973 and 1979 were particularly damaging to oil-importing countries. A run away from, or into, the currency may shock exchange rates away from simply reflecting differences in inflation between countries and so shock the system generally. At a stroke, so to speak, imports would have become much more expensive, to the disadvantage of consumers and wage earners and to the advantage of producers of goods competing with imports. Simultaneously, exports will have become more profitable again, to the advantage of producers and the disadvantage of consumers. The resulting devaluation then sets in motion enormous upward pressures on wages and prices generally. Once sent off in a new direction, the activity of the economy, as we have seen, gathers momentum and makes the essential self-adjustments until either the internal logic, or some new seismic event, sets it off in a new direction.

If the economy were easier to predict, the timing of important decisions would improve and this would mean less risk, more savings and investment, and so higher average growth rates and a better standard of living for all. With less variation in the growth rates, the progress of the economy would then depend even more on the supply side, on the encouragement provided to supply. There would less potential output lost as a result of the failure to anticipate the level of demand accurately.

The investment cycle

The most variable sectors of the economy are those that supply highly durable goods to the economy. The investment and durable goods cycles are far more variable than is the cycle for non-durable consumer goods. The more variable sectors obviously have more to contribute to the business cycle. If additional demand for investment and durable goods were less variable, then so would be their supply and the economy itself would be less variable and more predictable.

The more durable the goods or assets, the larger will be the available stocks of such assets, relative to their flows onto the market. New vehicle production each year in a mature economy, may be equivalent to no more than a tenth or twelfth of the total number of vehicles. New cars may be doing little more than simply replacing the cars that are being scrapped. Similarly, with bridges or office blocks, houses or steel mills, the established stocks of the asset are large, relative to the numbers produced annually. A small, up or down change in demand for the stock, will lead to large changes in demand in the construction, building and vehicle manufacturing industries. But such changes are difficult to predict and so the producers of cars and ships and bridges increase supplies in response to actual orders. They would be unable to survive should they attempt to maintain a stable level of output independently of actual demands. This would mean carrying large inventories of finished goods or reserves of machinery and labor, with which to try to make rapid adjustments to actual demand. And so they would rather play "catch up" and their supply responses lag behind demand and so help reinforce the income and output cycles.

What in fact is being observed and registered by the national income accountants, is supply rather than demand. Demand is being largely satisfied by the available stock of vehicles and buildings, and is reflected in their prices. In the case of the non-durable and service sectors of the economy, where by definition it is largely impossible to hold stocks, preferred demand and actual supply is much more closely matched. For this reason the output of non-durable production and services matches demand much more closely, and so reveals much more about what is in the minds of households than the investment good cycles. It tells us fairly directly about household perceptions of their wealth or the state of their balance sheets. They respond to strength or weakness in their balance sheets by increasing their demands for all goods and services. But only the demands for non-durables and services meet with a more or less immediate supply response.

The changes in supplies of and demands for non-durables appear quite random in character. This is because the information that changes the minds of households about their economic prospects, arrives in an unpredictable random way. The shocks to the system are random events, and they include the supply side shocks of discovery and invention, and the expected impact of changes in the rules and regulations applied by governments, that impact on wealth and on spending decisions. The shocks may be random, but the process of adjustment to them follows a more predictable pattern. Information about what consumers are actually spending on food and services tells us how they feel about the future. How consumers feel and act is obviously of great importance for the state of the economy.

1. The costs of hiring a worker or of the benefits of employment are more than money wages. They include the provision, by the employer, of medical insurance. This has become more expensive relative to all other goods and services and so has been an important factor holding down the growth in real money wages. The cost of medical insurance comes out of wages.

CHAPTER TWELVE
MONEY MATTERS

Monetary Policy

Reference has been made to monetary policy and the use central banks make of interest rate and money supply changes to influence demand. The interest rates that central banks control directly, are their own lending rates, that is, the rate of interest at which they are willing to supply cash directly to the banks. This is known as the discount or rediscount rate. This is because banks, when they raise cash this way, usually have to present the central bank with financial securities — typically, short dated government bills which will then be discounted for cash or which will serve as collateral for a central bank loan. The discount is the difference between the value of the asset at maturity, and the cash received today, which can be converted to a rate of interest or a discount rate. The central bank may also enter into a repurchase agreement with a borrowing bank. That is, agree to buy a security from the bank and sell it back later at a price agreed to now. This price then determines the repurchase or repossession rate.

The central bank also supplies cash to the system on its own initiative, by buying securities and foreign exchange from the banks and other financial institutions and dealers in the open market. It may also take up a new issue of government securities in exchange for cash.

If, as is often the case, the central bank acts as banker to the government, the supply of cash to the private sector will also increase as the government spends the proceeds of tax revenues or debt issues. As the government writes its cheques, cash flows out of the government account into bank accounts with the central bank. If the government departments are just another deposit account with the private banks, then, as with any bank customer, the cheques written on one account, in this case the government account, end up as deposits in another private account, usually with some other bank. There is then no outflow of cash from the banking system. The banking system also loses and gains cash when there is either a net inflow or outflow of notes from or to the banks' customers, or when the central bank buys or sells securities, or foreign exchange.

A central bank is almost always able to force the banks to ask for facilities, or generally to force up short-term rates of interest, by selling securities to the customers of the banks from its own portfolio. If the intention is to relieve upward pressure on short-term interest rates, the central bank may buy rather than sell securities, and so enable the banks to repay their loans to the central bank, or build up their cash reserves. The close links between the central bank and the commercial banks, and between these banks and all participants in financial markets, means that short-term rates of interest generally follow the lead given by the central bank. Long-term rates may or may not follow, depending on expectations of inflation. If the rise in short rates is taken to mean less inflation over the long term, long-term rates may well come down. even though short-term lending may have become more attractive.[1]

The origins of central banking

The essential power of the central bank rests in its monopoly of the supply of notes, granted to it by the government and by the deposits that banks are forced to keep with the central bank.

These deposits, together with the notes they hold, constitute the cash reserves of the banking system.

Central banks were originally given such powers over the money supply so that they would be able to act to prevent a financial crisis. This occurs when there is a crisis of confidence in the banks, or other financial institutions; and so deposit holders rush to the banks to demand their cash back. Banks, as are all borrowers who borrow short and lend longer, are vulnerable to a run for cash. A panic- induced demand to cash in deposits from one bank, can easily spread to all banks, even the most carefully managed ones. If so, the sudden attempts by all banks to get at cash, by calling in their loans and by selling other securities and assets which they hold, will cause a collapse in the value of all assets. These forced sales would have devastating effects on balance sheets generally, and so on the willingness and ability to spend. An economic crisis is bound to follow a major financial crisis.

A sudden loss of confidence in any financial institution or market will lead to withdrawals and forced sales of securities, forcing prices down. If the assets and liabilities are perfectly matched, as for example with a mutual fund that holds shares, then the value of the assets of the savers, which are the liabilities of the financial institution, decline at the same rate. Bankruptcy will not be threatened, but the decline in the wealth of the mutual fund holders may be very serious for the economy.

Central banks can prevent such an implosion of financial markets and their destructive influence on the real economy, by being able to supply unlimited supplies of cash when only cash will do to relieve the anxiety of depositors. This was the essential idea used to justify the establishment of central banks. The Federal Reserve Bank system of the USA was set up in 1913.[2] The first central bank, the Bank of England, was established as a private bank in the seventeenth century, when it was given a monopoly of the note issue in London. The Bank evolved its supportive central banking functions in the course of the nineteenth century, and so became the example other countries followed.

When deciding to protect the system as a lender of last resort, a central bank still has to exercise judgment about the terms upon which the relieving cash is supplied to the banks or other financial institutions in trouble. It will help most easily when it believes a bank, through no fault of its own, has been subject to a run inspired by some false rumour and when such a run threatens the whole system. If the bank has got itself into trouble through unwise lending practices, it may be inclined to protect the depositors for the sake of stabilizing the system, but is unlikely to want to protect the shareholders of the failed bank. But the central bank may also want depositors in general to be reminded of the wisdom of being cautious with their savings, with the result that sound banking practices are encouraged and lead to their appropriate rewards. Thus there is always a fine line to be drawn by the central bank between supporting the financial system or an individual bank in a time of crisis, while not encouraging imprudent banking and lending generally by doing so. This means in practice that the depositors in big banks, and sometimes their shareholders too, are too numerous and politically important to be made an example of. Smaller banks are much more vulnerable. So, until they get big enough, small banks have to be above reproach if they are to survive. This makes it much harder for them to compete with the big battalions for the public's cash.

Sometimes, as with the Savings and Loans crisis in the USA in the Eighties, the problems can get too big even for the money issuing powers of the central bank. The government's tax base was used to rescue depositors in the Savings and Loan banks, at a cost once estimated to be as much as US$200bn. These S&L's are the equivalent of building societies or mortgage banks, in other countries. In the USA, in addition to the support and surveillance function provided by the Federal Reserve Banking system, a system of compulsory deposit insurance protects small depositors against banking failures. It should be appreciated that regulation of banks in the USA has prevented the formation of a large branch banking network such as is found almost everywhere else. In the USA, the banking system consists of an extraordinary number of mostly small, deposit-taking banks.

The US government, in fact, had to rescue its own deposit insurance system from bankruptcy, because of the large numbers of failures of Savings and Loan banks. They failed, because they borrowed short at variable rates and lent long at fixed rates. As a result, when the inflation of the seventies, coupled with the deregulation of deposit rates, forced up short rates dramatically, it largely bankrupted the system. If banks could match the maturity structure of their liabilities and assets, they would be less exposed to risk. They would also then offer lower returns to their shareholders.

In addition, there were many examples of abuse of the system, on the "heads I win tails you lose" principle. Many S&Ls undertook reckless and sometimes fraudulent lending.[3] If the gambles succeeded, the owners would benefit. If they failed, the depositors were protected anyway. With none of their wealth assumed, correctly, to be at risk, the insured depositors did not have to concern themselves with the lending practices and solvency of their banks.

Power and power corrupted

Central banks, with their power to supply cash, can clearly help stabilize the system. But such power over the supply of money can obviously be abused by governments. Governments can avoid raising taxes, or raising interest rates to finance their expenditure, by getting their cash cheaply from the central bank – that is to say, by having the central bank print notes, or create deposits, in exchange for government bonds that offer an artificially low rate of interest. The conventional approach to the danger of governments inflating the money supply, is to attempt to entrench the independence of the central bank so that they can say "no" to governments and to higher inflation.

Another alternative, though one without any ground-swell in its favour, would be to allow competition in the issue of notes. If private banks were able to issue notes – as they once did, and did so prudently – and therefore avoided over-issuing their own notes, which it would be in their interest to do, it would be possible to substitute private for public money. If banks over-issued, they would have to convert their own excess notes into cash, or somebody else's notes. If the government were then to over-issue, the official currency would be devalued against private moneys. The rate of exchange of government into private money would decline. Such devaluations would perhaps have political consequences and discourage excesses by the government bank. More importantly, the availability of good substitutes for an inflating official currency would minimize the damage it causes. In times of high inflation, economic actors do turn away from domestic to foreign money, as both a way of transacting business and making contracts.

This is a form of competition between moneys usually inhibited by exchange controls. Clearly, a government that will resort to inflation is a government that will try and force its citizens to hold its own paper. Again, it comes back to the decisive political influences. Freedom from exchange control to hold and use a foreign currency, and freedom to issue substitutes for government money, may inhibit governments from resorting to printing money. But if governments are determined to issue money, because sound financial practices are too politically difficult for them to follow, nothing will stop them from doing so other than politics itself.

The transmission of monetary policy to the real economy

Central banks use interest rates to control the supply of money. They regard both interest rates, being the price of their cash, and the supply of cash and money, including bank deposits, as important for spending decisions. They may also indicate annual money supply targets that the bank is meant to achieve, by way of appropriate adjustments of interest rates. The typical money supply target is set by the central bank with the short-term outlook for the economy and inflation very much in mind. Higher growth targets are likely to be set if the economy needs help and lower if inflation is seen as the problem. If, then, actual money supply growth rates threaten to breach the target range, short-term interest rates will be increased. If money supply growth rates are tending to fall below the target, this would then call for lower interest rates to encourage demands for bank and other credit, and for cash. The threat to the money supply target may then be used as a leading indicator of interest rate changes.

The influence of interest rates on spending, through the cost of borrowing and the reward for saving, is perhaps obvious. The direct influence of money on spending is perhaps less so. Cash, or its close substitutes, cheque deposits at banks, are considered to be part of an appropriate mix of assets – part of the wealth portfolio. As they do with other components of their portfolio, households and firms will choose to hold just enough cash, or its equivalent, not too much and not too little, to facilitate their transactions in the market place for goods and services and for financial securities. Should the central bank introduce more cash into the system than they wish to hold, they get rid of the excess supply of cash in two ways. They either buy more goods and services, or they buy more financial assets. If they choose the first option, they affect the suppliers of goods and services directly. If they exchange their, now excess, money holdings for extra financial securities, they effect their prices and yields and investment and consumption demands indirectly, as discussed previously.

For this reason, changes in the supply of money have proved to be a very good leading indicator of the state of the economy and inflation. Any sustained increase in prices anywhere is associated with more money. Without an increase in the supply of money, increases in demand for goods that drive up prices cannot be sustained. Again, cause and effect must be clearly separated. If total demand rises because economic actors are getting rid of excess supplies of money, then given the limits placed on increasing the real supply of goods and services, prices must rise.

The rise in prices rations out the available supplies to those most willing to pay the price and so eliminates the excess supplies of money. With higher prices, firms and households need to increase their working stock of cash and so increase their demands to hold money accordingly. The process of rising prices would then end there, unless still more money is introduced into the system. If so, the process of rising prices continues. The opposite holds for a deflation, when prices in general are falling. If economic actors wish to hold more money, they will have to spend less in order to do so, and prices will fall until they are satisfied with their holdings of cash. Again it is not the quantity of money, but the real, or purchasing-power-adjusted quantity of money that counts. If the authorities wished to avoid falling prices, when the demand for money is increasing, they could supply more money to the system in order to satisfy the increased demands for money.

Money as a leading indicator

The relationship in the USA between the growth in the real *money base*, known as m0, and the real economy, is indicated in Figure 21. As may be seen, the turning points in the real money cycle often lead the turning points in the business cycle. Real money supply growth leads the economy out of the recession of 1981, and it falls back before the economy peaks in 1983. The turning point, signalling a recovery in 1990, was preceded by strong growth in real money in 1989 which was interrupted in late 1990. The recovery in the real money cycle then again resumed strongly in 1991 and 1992 and clearly helped to pull the economy firmly along with it in 1993. The great concern in early 1994 was about the inflationary potential of what became a very strong economic recovery which, it was assumed, could not

Fig. 21

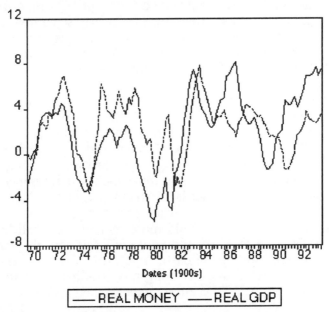

GROWTH IN REAL MONEY(m0) AND GDP

Dates (1900s)

REAL MONEY ── REAL GDP

190

continue at that pace. The brief set-back in money supply growth in 1990, indicated in the graph, can be held responsible for the hesitant recovery that dates from late 1991. The one recent period when the real money cycle would not have served as a good leading indicator of the state of the economy was in 1986. Then, economic growth rates declined, despite the previous recovery in the money cycle that began in 1984, and which only reversed itself in early 1987. It is perhaps of interest to note that the decline in real money growth in 1987 was interrupted briefly when the Federal Reserve Bank increased the supply of cash to counteract the stock market crash of October 1987. This was classic central bank intervention, but, as may be seen, was not enough to reverse a strong negative trend.

Given the involvement of central and other banks in the money supply system, the money supply shock that gets the money cycle going may well originate with the customers of banks, rather than with the central bank. Customers may wish to borrow more from their banks. The banks may then wish to satisfy them and will in turn borrow more cash from the central bank. If the central bank fails to anticipate this greater demand for cash, and so does not raise interest rates far enough, money supply growth will then accelerate in response to extra demands for cash from the banking system. It is quite possible for the central bank either to underestimate or overestimate the strength of the economy and so the demand for credit and, by not adjusting interest rates soon enough, this will reinforce the forces pushing the economy up or down. Then when the economic truth is known, the subsequent adjustment of interest rates, necessary to restore stability, will have to be a larger one.

Should the central bank be too optimistic about the state of the economy, interest rates would be set too high and the money supply would grow too slowly for the good of the economy. It should be recognized just how important it is that a central bank makes accurate forecasts of the state of the economy. If it is unable to do so, then its policies may prove to be highly destabilizing. It could be adding too much money when the economy is performing unexpectedly well, and too little should the central bank have forecast higher growth rates and demands for bank credit than in fact materialized.

We have concentrated the discussion here on the narrowest possible definition of money, being cash in the hands of the public or the banks. Bank deposits are a substitute for cash. The supply of commercial, or clearing bank deposits, is closely linked to the supply of cash made available to the system by the central bank. The supply of deposits can grow faster or slower than the supply of cash if the public comes to prefer notes to deposits or the other way round. Deposits may also grow faster or slower relative to the supply of cash if the banks reduce their own demands for cash or if the central bank allows them to do so by reducing the cash reserve requirements of banks. There are times, therefore, when a wider definition of money, one that includes bank deposits, may provide a better predictor of the state of the economy than the supply of cash, the so-called m0. This is defined as the notes issued by the central bank which are held by the non-bank public and the cash reserves, over and above those held as compulsory reserve requirements, held by the banks.[4] There are wider definitions of money, m1, m2 or m3, which are much larger than m0 because they include different categories of bank

Fig. 22

PREDICTING WIDER MONEY FROM NARROW MONEY

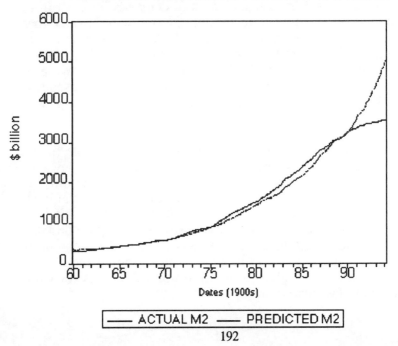

— ACTUAL M2 —— PREDICTED M2

deposits;[5] they may behave somewhat independently in the short run and give better predictions of the state of the economy. They may capture what is happening to the demand for money as well as the supply of money.

In Figure 22, we show the results of an equation that estimates m2 for the USA, using m0 as the independent or explanatory variable to predict m2. As may be seen, the fit is generally very close, though by the end of 1992, actual m2 had fallen below the levels predicted by m0. As a result, in 1992, m2 did not predict the recovery of the economy in 1993. Had close attention been paid to the trend in m0 over this period, the strong recovery of the economy would not have come as a surprise. m0 would have provided a very good leading indicator.

Any shift in the preferences of the public for shorter, rather than longer-dated deposits, will affect the relationship between the different m's. For this reason, m3 may grow faster or slower than m1 over any period, which will have no implications for the wider economy. The supply of narrow money would be a better predictor in such circumstances. Also, the banks may themselves wish to take on fewer (more) deposits and undertake more (less) of their activities off balance sheet, should regulations or circumstances change. The cash or capital reserve requirements of banks may make it less or more profitable for them to do so. Banks may act as agents rather than principals. When relatively more or less lending and borrowing is done off or on the balance sheets of banks, then this is called disintermediation, or reintermediation. Such shifts will affect the measures of money and so also disturb the links between money and economic activity.

Similarly, if the extra demands for cash come from foreigners who wish to use US dollars rather than, say, roubles, then any given increase in the supply of dollar notes – the largest part of narrow money by far – or in m0 will be less inflationary than otherwise for the US economy. As indicated, it is the excess of the supply of money over the demand for money that matters for prices or output, and not the supply of money itself. Economy watchers need to be aware of both sides of this important equation.

In Figure 23, the results of a regression equation for the USA,

Fig. 23

USING NARROW MONEY TO PREDICT THE PRICE LEVEL

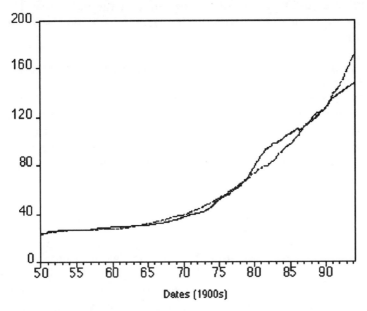

Dates (1900s)

| —— PRICE LEVEL (87=100) —— PREDICTED PRICE LEVEL |

that estimates the level of prices as a function of the level of the narrow money supply, is shown. As may be seen, the fit is a very good one, with an R squared of over 0.98. It may also be seen that using narrow money as a predictor of inflation would have led to underestimates of inflation in the early Eighties and over-estimates in the early Nineties. Thus we need to predict changes in both the supply of and demands for money. The difference between supply and demand for money will bring either more or less inflation, or more or less output growth. Depending on the state of the economy, and inflationary expectations, a condition more or less of one or the other will arise. If the economy is already operating close to full capacity, then much of the impact of the excess supplies of money, and so extra spending, must be on prices and wages. If the economy has excess capacity, then output and employment may increase ahead of prices and wages.

The natural rate of unemployment

Much attention in economic analysis has been concentrated upon measuring the so-called *natural rate of employment*, or output. That is the rate which, if exceeded, will mean the onset of inflationary pressures. In the longer run, the rate of inflation will largely reflect the difference between the actual growth in the money supply and the potential growth in the economy. In other words, the demand for money to hold is likely to grow in line with the real economy. Thus, an economy with more growth potential can tolerate a more rapid increase in the supply of money without igniting inflation. Any improvements in payments technology, for example the wider use of bank cards as alternative methods of payment, or easier access to bank machines, which enable people to carry less cash or firms to manage their cash more effectively, will gradually reduce the demand for money. The rate at which the money supply should then be allowed to grow in order to put neither inflationary nor deflationary pressure on the economy, would then have to be adjusted accordingly.

Supply and demand once more

In the short run, for the reasons indicated, if such changes were not completely anticipated, changes in the money supply itself may effect prices or real output or some mixture of them. While the size of the money supply and the level of prices will always be highly correlated in all countries, the time lag between changes in money supply and changes in the level of prices is likely to be variable. In small, open economies, capital flows may cause the nominal exchange rate to change, which in turn will influence the inflation rate independently of money supply growth. That is, in the short run – over which price level changes are measured –*supply side shocks* may be responsible for changes in the price level. Money supply changes influence the level of demand in the economy directly. There are also independent forces, for example a drought or a flood, as well as an oil price shock or an exchange rate change, that reduce the supply of goods and push up prices. And so the supply side effects may predominate for a while. But in any long-run view of the causes of inflation, the long run being longer than two years in this case, inflation may be regarded as always and everywhere a monetary phenomenon. [6] That is, prices generally will not be able to rise in a sustained way unless the money supply continues to increase.

There is a common confusion about the links between productivity and inflation. Clearly, any improvement in the productivity of the labour force or capital stock will mean more output, more supplies. Were other forces acting on prices to remain unchanged, the price level, and so inflation rates, would fall. In such circumstances, any increase in productivity would cause prices to rise at a slower rate. Given the nature of things, however, the scope for productivity increases are limited. If the productivity of the labour force is improving by 2 to 3 % a year, an economy is doing very well. But inflation may be anything from zero to an infinite amount, because there are no technical limits to how fast a government can print money. Unless government restrains itself, no feasible quantum of increases in productivity or efficiency are going to make much difference to high inflation rates – that is to say – those above 5% per annum. Wishful thinking about productivity will not get rid of inflation. Only the right kinds of monetary policy will do that – which of course takes the right kind of politics.

1. In the USA between 1980 and 1992 the correlation statistic for monthly changes in short and long rates was .67. That is to say, on average, short and long rates move together nearly 70% of the time.
2. It is strongly argued that the Federal Reserve System hopelessly failed its most important test, which was to prevent the collapse of the US banking system after the great New York stock market crash of 1929. A third of all US banking deposits

were lost between 1929 and 1933 as bank after bank folded. This loss of wealth clearly contributed to the great depression of the thirties. It also made the surviving banks very cautious lenders, concerned more with building up cash reserves than lending them out. See Milton Friedman, *The Great Contraction, 1929–1933,* Princeton, Princeton University Press, 1965.

3. Fundamentally, the system broke down because inflation and short-term interest rates rose. The controls on short-term deposit rates, which had protected the S&L's against competition, had to be abandoned in the face of rising, market-determined short-term interest rates. One way for the S&L's to avoid slow strangulation was to take higher risks for higher returns.

4. It should be emphasized that subtracting cash held as reserve requirements by the banks is adjusting in part for the demand for cash reserves by the banks. If this adjustment were not made, then when the cash reserve requirements imposed on banks were increased, this would show up as an increase in the supply of m0 and could be misinterpreted as monetary expansion. Again, it is the excess supply of money that counts.

5. The larger the subscript, the wider the definition of money. For example in the USA, m1 comprises the sum of currency, travellers cheques, demand deposits and other checkable deposits. m2 is m1 plus overnight repurchase agreements and overnight Eurodollars, money market mutual funds and money market deposit accounts and savings and small time deposits. m3 is m2 plus large time deposits, term repurchase agreements and term Eurodollars.

6. This phrase I associate with Milton Friedman, the most eminent of the modern monetarists who are literally those who, like myself, think money (money supply) matters – though the term is applied more widely to those who argue the case for market forces, rather than government intervention. Not all market loving economists are monetarists in the narrow sense described here. For a review of Friedman's latest work on money see his *Money Mischief, Episodes in Monetary History,* New York, Harcourt Brace, Javanovich, 1992.

CHAPTER THIRTEEN

PLAYING THE ECONOMIC GAME, TAKING EVASIVE ACTION AND FIRING BACK

Much of this book has emphasized the importance of knowing what the economic future holds and how it might be read with advantage. This final chapter concentrates on the role played by economic expectations and the implications of this for economic policy.

Inflationary and other expectations

The relationship between total spending and the level of prices / output is much complicated by inflationary expectations. Prices and wages negotiated between firms, workers, managers and trade unions, do not simply respond to actual demand, which is known to be influenced by monetary policy, but anticipate it. If spending turns out largely as expected, because monetary policy has behaved as anticipated, there would be no further need for firms to adjust output or employment levels, or for wages or prices to adapt. The prices and wages that have been negotiated will prove to be at their appropriate levels. If, however, prices or wages were set too optimistically, and levels of demands for goods and labour proved disappointingly weak, there would be pressure to adjust wages and prices. Firms would be inclined to cut prices and job offers to encourage more demand and to reduce costs. If the level of spending had been underestimated, because the firms and their suppliers were too pessimistic about the state of the economy, the opposite effects on prices and wages and on output and employment would occur. Prices and wages would tend to rise more rapidly, as would output.

And so, especially in higher-inflation countries, we tend to see stagflation, that is, high or higher inflation associated with slow or slower growth. There is thus no simple relationship between growth and actual inflation. In fact there is no evidence of any trade-off between them for the USA, as may be seen in Figure 24. If anything, more inflation is associated with slower, rather than faster growth in output and employment.[1]

Because it is in the interest of all economic decision makers, including firms, trade unions and participants in financial markets, to be well informed about inflation trends among other influences on their economic welfare, inflation, once anticipated, will not have predictable effects on the growth cycle. Unexpectedly low or high inflation will, however, do so. Some view of inflation is in the plans of business and households and will be reflected in interest, wage and exchange rates and in the prices of assets. Unexpectedly low inflation will disappoint these plans, and as part of the process of adjustment of actual to expected inflation, output and employment growth will decline. This is what makes bringing down inflation, when inflationary expectations are so well entrenched, such an uncomfortable business. Similarly, if inflation is underestimated, the unexpectedly higher actual inflation will temporarily stimulate more output and employment. The link between higher inflation and the lower unemployment rate indicated in Figure 24 (c) for the USA, between 1950 and 1969, occurred when inflation was low and was expected to remain low. Increases in the actual rate of inflation over this period, may well be regarded as equivalent to an unexpected increase in the rate of inflation.

Fig. 24a   INFLATION AND GROWTH IN EMPLOYMENT

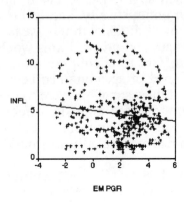

EM PGR

Fig. 24b

INFLATION AND UNEMPLOYMENT RATE 1960-1994

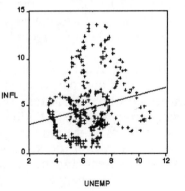

UNEMP

Fig. 24c   INFLATION AND UNEMPLOYMENT 1950-1969

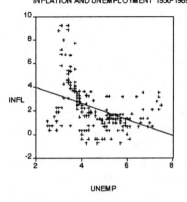

UNEMP

If everybody could accurately predict the level of demand in the economy, prices would be set accurately in anticipation of demand and inflation would have no real effects. But when prices are set too low, because inflationary pressure has been underestimated, firms and workers react as if the real demand for their goods and labor has increased. They therefore supply more at prevailing prices. If they have overestimated demand, and set prices too high when actual demand is disappointingly low, they reduce supplies to the market. For this reason, unexpectedly high inflation is a stimulus, and unexpectedly low inflation is a depressant for the economy. Governments may therefore be tempted into destroying their credibility. That is, having got people to believe that inflation is under control, they may then take advantage of these beliefs to pump in more money, to give the economy a popular boost.

The problem with inflation

Inflation itself, as opposed to inflationary surprises, does no good, but harm to the economy. It does so because it raises the risks of taking economic action. It makes real prices more difficult to predict, because not all prices ever rise at the same rate. The price of timber relative to the price of furniture, or the price of cars relative to the price of steel or plastic, or wages compared to rents, becomes more variable with higher inflation. This adds to business risks. Lenders and borrowers, especially, become more uncertain about the costs of borrowing and the rewards for lending. Importers and exporters will find it more difficult to plan ahead, because exchange rates are unlikely simply to compensate for higher or lower inflation in the countries with whom they trade. In all these ways, inflation becomes an uncomfortable part of economic life with which businesses and households attempt to cope as best they can by building inflationary expectations into their plans.

Not the least of the extra risks to which they will be exposed is the risk of the government dealing popularly with the symptoms, rather than the causes of the inflation. Wage and price controls, subsidies and penalties, exchange control and interest controls, as well as interference with the indexes that are used to adjust automatically for inflation in contracts, can be expected, as inflation runs its course. Businesses can easily find themselves severely disadvantaged by such developments.

Expectations and policy

It is recognition of the role in the economy played by expectations, rather than practical grounds alone, which has undermined the case for fine-tuning the economy. Such recognition is the essential part of the case for rules for policy makers. If economic actors are well informed, and attempt to anticipate policy actions, then for all the reasons indicated here, policy actions, if they are to be effective, must take the economy by surprise. There is no reason to believe that the surprise will be of the happy kind that will achieve the objective of faster growth on average. The economy is a moving target, and only too capable of firing back. Hitting the moving target means being prepared to take evasive action. Helping the economy along becomes a game, which the government can only win by doing the unexpected. So efforts to understand what governments are actually up to – to judge them by what they do, and not what they say and so to take evasive or opportunistic action – remain highly appropriate.

Serious economists have not been able to disregard the significance of expectations for their models of how the economy works. Those who continue to believe in fine-tuning rely upon the existence of time-lags in the adjustment process, of rigid prices, and especially of inflexible wages, particularly in the downward direction, to justify government intervention. The more rigid wages and prices are, the longer it will take the labor and other markets to react to weaker demand. When aggregate demand declines, price and wage rigidities result in more excess capacity and unemployment. If the economic system operated more like an auction, market prices would adapt rapidly to excess supply and demand and the economy would operate much closer on average to its full employment potential. Thus economists build models with so-called rational expectations[2] and with rigid prices, and can show that, because prices and wages react slowly, governments, even given rational expectations, can potentially speed the process of adjustment along.

So, playing the game of fine-tuning remains both intellectually respectable and practically important. Given the difficulties in forecasting the state of the economy, there remains a constant tension between too little and too much spending, whatever state the economy is in. There will always be those, inside and outside government, who, even when the economy is booming, will be worried most about how an increase in interest rates will affect the health of the economy. In recessions, there will be those emphasizing the dangers of inflation, because too much money is being pumped into the economy. There is always the worry that the authorities will be behind the curve. Too little too late, and the economy booms away for a while longer. This in turn may lead to a reaction of too much, too late, and the economy slides more rapidly into recession.

Final reservations about the role of governments in the economy

Normally, more government spending means less private spending, as has been indicated above. Governments have either to tax more or borrow more of the available savings, so crowding out private spending. But in times of recession there is no private spending to be crowded out. The alternative to more government spending at such times may be less spending generally. Therefore during recessions, extra well-timed government spending would not involve any sacrifice of private spending. It has no resource cost and should help get private spending going again. The economic problem, so to speak, has been suspended. The problem is one of too little demand, rather than of too little supply. When private spending does get going again, the idea is that the government should then cut back in order to make room for it.

The role for government, in dealing with a deep recession, seems obvious enough to economists trained in, and convinced of, the Keynesian approach to demand management. It is simply for the government to spend the economy out of that recession. That, however, largely begs the question as to why the economy got into its depressed state in the first place. The role played by the government in causing the crisis, in undermining the confidence of the heads of households and private firms, and so their willingness to spend, is likely to have been important in causing the recession. So, unless the root cause of the crisis is successfully addressed, more government spending may not do much good.

The extra incomes earned by doing business with government may be saved or sent abroad. If investors react negatively to government action, they will withdraw more capital and put further pressure on the exchange rate. This will exert upward pressure on prices generally, which will subtract further from the ability to spend more. Locally owned enterprises may seek greener pastures elsewhere in the world, as may the most highly skilled workers and best-educated members of the professions.

Regaining the confidence of the private sector may require, therefore, that, even in a recession, the government demonstrates its willingness to act in the best interests of the economy in the long run, by for example bringing down inflation. This goes altogether against the instinctive grain, given the importance of sustaining demand. Once inflation is well entrenched, it is just as likely that a recession will come with it, rather than instead of it, for reasons dealt with below. Such problems may mean government taking action which is the reverse of trying to spend the economy out of recession. It might mean, for example, balancing the budget by reducing government spending and raising taxes; or increasing interest rates and reducing money supply growth. There would seem no obvious and always best way for governments to deal with a deep recession, other than not to get into such difficulties in the first place. This they can do by sustaining a confidence building set of policies.

Getting the timing right, fine-tuning the economy by way of small appropriate adjustments to government spending and taxes, as the majority of economists would have governments do, is in practice a very difficult task. Not only must the authorities be very good economic forecasters, but they must also have to be able to adjust their spending and taxing plans at very short notice in response to the changing state of the economy. Such powers are unlikely to be delegated by politicians to technocrats at the Ministry for Stabilizing the Economy, for good political reasons.

They know they will be held politically responsible for changes in taxation and spending priorities, and it will be very difficult to isolate the impact of, and responsibility for, business cycle relief, or impositions from the budget in general. They know also, that it is not so much government spending in general that matters to their re-election, but spending in particular ways and in particular districts. They are also well aware of the unpopularity of taxes.

Such concerns make the government budget a long drawn out process, not at all suited to fine-tuning. Also, by the time the budgets are agreed, the economic conditions are likely to have changed significantly. There is no scope there for fine-tuning. In the USA, the President presents budget proposals in February. A budget is agreed upon by September, which will then apply until the following September.

In countries where spending and tax powers are more concentrated with the government of the day, which enjoys a clear majority in parliament or the like, governments can be confident of having their budgets passed at short notice. In such systems, there is more scope for expansionary budgets, should the economy need a boost. Raising taxes or cutting spending, should either be necessary for stabilization-policy reasons, will still be as unpopular as they are for any other purpose.

Conclusion

It is clearly important for all those affected by economic policy to anticipate what the government will do. Simply hoping for something better, will not be good enough. Realistic judgments are called for if private incomes and wealth are to be protected, as effectively as possible, from the failures of government policy. All governments, in their economic policy, will be tempted to trade off what may be longer-run damage caused to economic prospects, for the achievement of short-run advantages. Before the long run is established, we may not only be dead, but (from the politicians' perspective, something almost as bad) they may be out of office. Clearly, not all governments succeed in taking enough of a long-run view. They are not all able to avoid the temptation of the quick fix, that creates major problems, to which politically difficult adjustments may or may not be made later.

Successful economies are, by definition, those that have been able to avoid many of the potential excesses of policy. Or, if they have erred, they have also been able to make the appropriate adjustments in a more or less timely way. By so doing, they have provided a more stable economic environment, which encourage savings and investment, enterprise and economic growth.

How business must play the economic, or rather the economist's game

The game is therefore one of predicting what governments will do. Will they adopt more inflationary policies, or not? Having done so, will they reverse course later, or is the outlook one of still higher inflation in the future? In the latter case, the issue then becomes one of how the government will respond. Will it resort to price/wage/import and export controls? Will it introduce exchange and capital market controls and so on? The possibilities are endless and the rewards for realism and vigilance by the successful operator can be enormous, even if the policies undertaken are highly damaging to the economy generally. There are economies that make it back from what everybody thought was the abyss.

It is important to know who is setting the policy agenda and their particular model of the economy. It is necessary to keep a sharp eye out for possible changes in the agenda resulting from changes within the ruling government, as well as for the possibility of changes in the government itself.

Behind the policy reactions of the authorities responsible for economic policy, will be some theory of economic cause and effect employed by political leaders and their officials. Their beliefs about how the economy works will clearly be influenced by one or other school of economic thought. Success in the market place and in financial and commodity markets, more immediately than in other markets, will depend not only on a knowledge of how the economy works, but also on how the people responsible for economic policy believe the economy works. The accuracy of their beliefs is perhaps less important than the beliefs themselves. Thus, practical men and women will leave fine arguments about economics to the professors of economics. They are right to be less concerned with truth than with which ideas are currently winning. Ideas mean policy agendas, and these agendas will have profound implications for the economy.

In a perverse way, the less predictable the economy in general and the more the government interferes with it, the greater the rewards for a lucky or gifted few. Risk and returns do go together. A bold or lucky few can thrive by managing risk successfully. Often this means managing the politicians and officials who are fundamentally responsible for the risky environment in the first place. Sometimes the smart operators succeed by bribing the politicians and officials with power over the economy. More often, they succeed by being their good friends, being influential, which may not involve breaking the law.

A final sermon for well-meaning politicians and those who elect them

The more predictable the economic environment and the more certain economic actors are about the rules of the game, the more competition there will be to take advantage of the perceived opportunities. This competition, to participate in a favourable economic environment, will reduce profit margins to the advantage of consumers. It will increase the demands for, and the rewards of, workers and managers. Firms will take the longer-term view. With the greater confidence they have in securing the returns and rewards they hope to achieve, the firms will want to commit themselves to the future by investing more in plant and equipment, and in education, training and research. They may be more willing to borrow more, while local and foreign savers prove more eager to lend to them. All of which makes for a faster rate of economic growth and, for the deprived inhabitants of undeveloped countries, the opportunity to transform their economic prospects and those of their children, as, indeed, prospects in the developed countries have already been transformed.

The key ingredients for sustained economic advances are no mystery. It simply takes good government, which largely means good management of their economy. And in the recipe for economic growth, less does very largely mean more. It is not difficult to recognize the signs of good, or improving, economic management. And financial markets will be the first to give approval. Yet they are as ready to sell a country as they are a firm, when they expect economic conditions to deteriorate.

The returns from policies which do right by the economy, by providing the right environment and which provide an encouraging mix of rewards for economic effort, could not be greater over the long term – perhaps a generation. As has now been proved in a great many cases, they mean longer, more comfortable lives for the huge majority of the people. How much psychological benefit they gain, from affluence and the opportunity to fill minds as well as stomachs, remains the responsibility of the individual. If governments get it wrong, it threatens the economic well-being of all. In those countries that have barely got started on the road to greater prosperity, if governments do badly, all but a few, usually the few working for and controlling the government, continue to be ground down by poverty. Life for them will remain largely a crude struggle to survive.

It remains a mystery why, in so many countries, it is so difficult for people to get the good economic management they surely deserve. Perhaps if they all knew more economics, or had a better sense of economic history, the people, and the governments they elect, or who represent them, would be able to take the long view and so avoid the temptation for a popular quick fix that proves so damaging to economic prospects. Sadly, those who know the damage wrong policies can cause and have options available, still continue to act accordingly, perhaps saving themselves, but, by their actions cause irreparable economic damage to the economy and the people they leave behind.

The wealth of nations depends on the provision of a framework of laws and institutions which allows people, more or less, to get on with their work, and which provides economic rewards or incomes that, as closely as possible, reflect the contributions they have made. The value of such contributions is, ideally, measured by incomes earned through a process of voluntary exchange between participants in a free market in which newcomers can enter and compete. Opportunities and incomes should not have to depend directly, to any important extent, on commands or orders issued by government officials. Where governments do get involved, as buyers of goods or hirers of labor, they should do so in as obviously meritocratic a way as possible. Economically successful societies will be more tolerant of unequal rewards for unequal efforts because they are more easily recognized as fairly earned. Perhaps this book has made it easier to recognize those economies where more favourable conditions are in place, and those where there is a danger of them falling out of place. The creation and protection of the wealth of individuals calls for a great deal of vigilance.

1. Such relationships between output or employment growth and prices or wage rates, are known as Phillips' curves, after their originator A. W. Phillips, who identified a negative relationship between changes in money wages and the unemployment rate in Britain between 1861 and 1957. It is this relationship that appears to have broken down. The closest thing to a Phillips' curve here, is the the positive association between inflation and the unemployment rate found in the USA between 1950 and 1969.
2. Rational expectations are defined as the expectations derived from the economic model. That is, economic actors build models and make predictions based upon them as do economists, only more formally. The predictions derived from manipulating the models then constitute rational expectations. Of course, neither all economists nor all practitioners agree on what constitutes the appropriate view of the world that is incorporated in the model. But competition between models and the economic actors who use them is decided by the survival of the better models. The most highly credited members of the Rational Expectations school, are Robert Lucas of Chicago University and Thomas Sargent of the Hoover Institution.

INDEX OF ECONOMIC TERMS

INDEX

Added-value, sharing in, 22
Africa, 6
Argentina, 88
Australia, 88

Balance of Payments, 74ff.
  calculation, 76–7
Balance sheets and financial ratios,
175–7
Bank of England, 61, 185
Bank of France, 61
Bank of Germany, Central, see
Bundesbank
Belgium, 61, 100
Berlin Wall, 62
Booms and recessions, 178–80
Borrowing, 174-4
Bretton Woods Conference, 64n
Britain, Great, see UK
Bundesbank, 62, see also
Deutschmark
Bush, George, 168
Business cycle, diagnosis of, 165ff.

Canada, 105
Capital, cost of, see Cost of capital
Capitalists, 43
Cash flows, importance of, 174–5
Central Bank of Germany, see
Bundesbank

Central banking, origins of, 184ff.
Change, economic, positive

realiztion of, 20ff.
China, 88, 164
Citibank economic database, 64n
Clinton Administration, USA, 102
Clinton, Bill, 100, 103, 168
Common Market, see EEC
Competition: demand side of, 33ff.;
nature of, 24ff.; policies against,
28ff.
Congress Office of the Budget, USA,
102
Consumption, 90ff.; explosion of,
24ff.
Constant prices, 83
Cost of capital: 112–113; and tax
rates, 113ff.
Cost/price gap closure, 22ff.; case
study of, 31ff.
CPI, 66ff., 162, 137

Dallas, Texas, 118
D mark, see Deutschmark
Deficits, fiscal and trade relation-
ships, 75–6
Department of Justice, USA, 35n
Derivatives, 146ff.
Deutschmark, 61, 62, 153, 154
Dividends, 137ff.
Dollar standard, 63
Dollar, US, see US dollar

Economic analysis, 36ff.
Economic choices, 3ff.

212

Structural adjustment programme of
IMF, 74
Subsidies, and taxes, 117ff.
Swaps, 146ff.
Sweden, 94, 105

Taxes and subsidies, valuing, 117ff.
Tax rates vs revenues, 50ff.
Taxation limits, 96–7
Third World, 6, 47
Tobin, James, 129n
Tokyo Stock Exchange, 145, 162
Trade deficit, causes of, 77–8
Trade-offs, 1ff.
Trade policies, 161ff.

UK, 26, 61, 62, 82, 91, 104, 105, 179
Unemployment rate, natural, 195
USA, passim, *see* also US dollar;
New York Stock Exchange
US dollar, 59, 77, 78, 92, 153, 156ff.,
164, 193
USSR, 164

Value-added, calculation of, 70
Vietnam War, 60

Wages and employment, 172ff.
Wall Street, 126, *see* also New York
Stock Exchange
Wealth and welfare, 99ff.
World Bank, 161
World Trade Organization, 17n, 116

Yen, 158, 161, 164,
see also Tokyo Stock Exchange